KT-178-524

USBORNE GUIDE TO
TREES
OF BRITAIN & EUROPE

MARY BARRETT

Contents

Introduction	3
Leaf Key	4
Crown and Trunk Shapes	6
Bark Characteristics	7
Flowers and Fruits	8
Seasonal Variations in Trees	8
Seasonal Changes in Beech	9
The Field Guide	10
Further Reading	126
Useful Addresses	126
Index of English Names	127
Index of Scientific Names	128

Editorial Director Sue Jacquemier

Series Editor Rick Morris

Editor Diana Shipp

Designer David Bennett

Illustrators Annabel Milne, Peter Stebbing, Bob Bampton

Additional artwork by Denise Finney, David More, Norma Burgin, Delyth Jones, Sheila Galbraith, Wendy Bramall, Andy Martin

A number of the illustrations in this book have been previously published in the Usborne Spotter's Guides series.

First published in 1981 by Usborne Publishing Limited, 20 Garrick Street, London WC2E 9BJ

Printed and bound in Great Britain by Fakenham Press Limited, Fakenham, Norfolk.

Introduction

This book is a guide to the identification of some of the trees of Britain and Europe, and is intended primarily for use in the field. The trees are grouped into broadleaves and conifers, with two 'oddities' – Yew and Maidenhair Tree – at the end. The species are arranged by family. (Trees within a family share a similar flower structure – this is the basis of a botanical classification – and frequently have other features, such as fruits and leaf shapes, in common.) Similar-looking trees therefore generally appear on consecutive pages. The order of the families follows, for the main part, *Flora Europaea* (ed. Tutin *et al*).

The Illustrations

For each tree, there is a large colour illustration of the leaf and bark, and included in this image are the flowers and fruits if they are distinctive. At the top of each page is a colour illustration of the tree in full leaf and, for deciduous trees, a silhouette of the tree in winter. Additional illustrations show leaves, bark, flowers and fruits at varying stages of development, winter twigs and other distinctive features. Occasionally, similar species or varieties are illustrated in a small panel.

The Text

The text at the foot of each page gives details of the places in which the tree is likely to grow, whether it is native or introduced, its geographical distribution in the British Isles and notes on similar species. At the top of each page an introductory paragraph describes the shape and style of growth of the tree and summarizes the most distinctive features for identification. The text around the illustrations points out the main features of each part of the tree. The time of the year when the flowers, fruits, etc. can be seen appears beside each image. This period may vary slightly from year to year and in the extreme north and south of the British Isles. Comparisons with other trees are included both in the introductory paragraph and under the heading *Similar species*, and also, where appropriate, in a special panel headed *Do not confuse*. The scientific names used are from *Flora Europaea*.

Measurements

Measurements are given in both metric and imperial terms, the imperial figure being the nearest convenient estimate to the more exact metric figure. The measurements which appear after the scientific name refer to the height of an average, open-grown, mature specimen. This height figure is intended only as a guide since a tree's growth is, of course, dependent on its age and the situation in which it is growing.

Tree Distribution

Introduced trees have been deliberately planted and—unless they are naturalized—are confined to parks, gardens, roadsides or plantations. Many native trees are also planted for a variety of purposes, from forestry to landscaping. Geographical distribution and abundance of trees is related to habitat, soils and climate. In order of decreasing abundance, trees are described in this book as being *common, frequent, locally abundant,* or *rare*. The term *locally abundant* means that a tree is restricted to particular areas or localised concentrations.

The Selection of Species

In selecting the species for this book we have included almost all our native species and the most commonly planted introduced trees. We have also included examples of our rarer trees, such as Olive and European Hop-hornbeam, with the aim of showing the beauty and diversity of our tree flora.

LEAF KEY

This key will help you locate a tree in the book when you are working from a leaf specimen. The key is based on the shape and arrangement of leaves. Before using the key read the explanation opposite which explains what to look for when selecting a leaf. See also the explanation of simple and compound leaves.

Long, narrow leaves	Evergreen, oval leaves	Deciduous, oval leaves	Heart-shaped or Ace-of-spades leaves	Round leaves	Broad, lobed leaves	Oval, lobed leaves
		Bay Willow 13				
		Goat Willow 14				
		Silver Birch 22				
		Downy Birch 23				
		Grey Alder 25				
		Hornbeam 26				
		European Hop-hornbeam 27			White Poplar 16	
		Raoul 29			Grey Poplar 17	
		Beech 30			Tulip Tree 43	
		Sweet Chestnut 31			London Plane 46	
		English Elm 38			Oriental Plane 47	
		Wych Elm 39			Swedish Whitebeam 53	
		Smooth-leaved Elm 40	Black Poplar 19		Wild Service Tree 54	
		Crab Apple 48	Silver Birch 22		Hawthorn 56	
		Apple 49	Downy Birch 23		Midland Hawthorn 57	
	Holm Oak 36	Pear 50			Sycamore 72	
	Cork Oak 37	Whitebeam 52			Norway Maple 73	English Oak 32
	Evergreen Magnolia 42	Blackthorn 58	Black Mulberry 41		Field Maple 74	Sessile Oak 33
	Sweet Bay 44	Bird Cherry 59	Common Lime 80	Grey Poplar 17	Smooth Japanese Maple 75	Turkey Oak 34
White Willow 10	Box 45	Wild Cherry 60	Small-leaved Lime 81	Aspen 18	Guelder Rose 93	Red Oak 35
Weeping Willow 11	Portugal Laurel 64	Sour Cherry 61	Large-leaved Lime 82	Common Alder 24	Maidenhair Tree 125	Holm Oak 36
Crack Willow 12	Cherry Laurel 65	Plum 62	Silver Lime 83	Hazel 28		Swedish Whitebeam 53
Common Osier 15	Holly 78	Almond 63	Lilac 89	Judas Tree 69		Holly 78
Olive 88	Cider Gum 84	Japanese Cherry 66	Indian Bean Tree 90	Cider Gum (young tree) 84		
	Strawberry Tree 85	Spindle 79				
		Wayfaring Tree 92				

Long, narrow leaves	Evergreen, oval leaves	Deciduous, oval leaves	Heart-shaped or Ace-of-spades leaves	Round leaves	Broad, lobed leaves	Oval, lobed leaves
More than 5 times as long as they are broad	Usually thick, leathery and glossy; 2-3 times as long as they are broad	Usually thinner and softer; 2-3 times as long as they are broad	Broad based with pointed tip	May have notched or pointed tips	Roughly hand-shaped with pointed or rounded lobes	Oval outline with pointed or rounded lobes

4

When using the key try to choose a mature, representative leaf, bearing in mind that leaves are often very variable, even on one tree. If the tree has needle-like leaves note how they are arranged: are they held singly, or arranged in bunches, pairs or rows? If the tree has oval, undivided leaves, decide if they are evergreen (thick and leathery), or deciduous (thinner and softer). Some trees have two kinds of leaves or have very variable leaves, so appear in more than one category.

To use the key, first decide on the shape of your leaf according to the categories listed at the bottom of these pages. Above each leaf category is a list of trees with leaves of that shape and the number of the page on which each tree appears. Turn to the pages indicated to determine which species you have. For ease of reference, broadleaved trees are on a light green background; conifers and Yew are on a darker green background.

Simple and compound leaves

All conifers have needle-like leaves or scale-like leaves. Broadleaved trees may have simple or compound leaves. Compound leaves have many leaflets which may be arranged on each side of a stalk (pinnate), or radiating from a central point (palmate). To decide if you have a compound leaf, look for its buds. There is a bud at the base of every leaf stalk, never at the base of a leaflet.

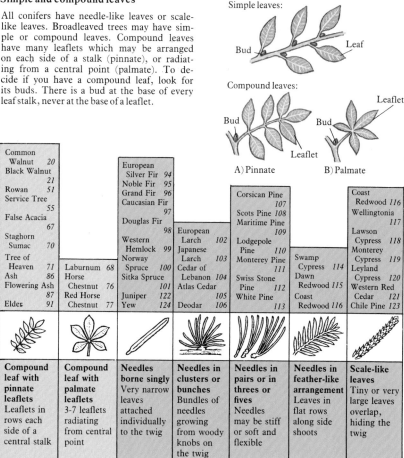

Simple leaves:

Bud   Leaf

Compound leaves:

Leaflet

Bud   Bud

Leaflet

A) Pinnate   B) Palmate

Compound leaf with pinnate leaflets	Compound leaf with palmate leaflets	Needles borne singly	Needles in clusters or bunches	Needles in pairs or in threes or fives	Needles in feather-like arrangement	Scale-like leaves
Common Walnut 20		European Silver Fir 94				Coast Redwood 116
Black Walnut 21		Noble Fir 95				Wellingtonia 117
Rowan 51		Grand Fir 96		Corsican Pine 107		
Service Tree 55		Caucasian Fir 97		Scots Pine 108		Lawson Cypress 118
False Acacia 67		Douglas Fir 98	European Larch 102	Maritime Pine 109		Monterey Cypress 119
Staghorn Sumac 70		Western Hemlock 99	Japanese Larch 103	Lodgepole Pine 110		Leyland Cypress 120
Tree of Heaven 71	Laburnum 68	Norway Spruce 100	Cedar of Lebanon 104	Monterey Pine 111	Swamp Cypress 114	Western Red Cedar 121
Ash 86	Horse Chestnut 76	Sitka Spruce 101	Atlas Cedar 105	Swiss Stone Pine 112	Dawn Redwood 115	Chile Pine 123
Flowering Ash 87	Red Horse Chestnut 77	Juniper 122	Deodar 106	White Pine 113	Coast Redwood 116	
Elder 91		Yew 124				

Compound leaf with pinnate leaflets	Compound leaf with palmate leaflets	Needles borne singly	Needles in clusters or bunches	Needles in pairs or in threes or fives	Needles in feather-like arrangement	Scale-like leaves
Leaflets in rows each side of a central stalk	3-7 leaflets radiating from central point	Very narrow leaves attached individually to the twig	Bundles of needles growing from woody knobs on the twig	Needles may be stiff or soft and flexible	Leaves in flat rows along side shoots	Tiny or very large leaves overlap, hiding the twig

Crown and Trunk Shapes

All trees of the same species have a characteristic shape but this can vary according to where the tree is growing. An oak tree growing in an isolated position in parkland will have a short, stout trunk and a broad, spreading crown. An oak tree growing in a wood will have a longer, thinner trunk and a much narrower crown. In addition, most trees become broader as they age. The shape of a tree can also be affected by cutting. Two examples of this are coppicing and pollarding, traditional practices for obtaining wood for fuel or fencing.

The illustrations below show some of the variations found in crowns and trunks. These are useful to note when trying to identify a tree.

Crowns

Broad, spreading
e.g. English Oak

Broad with high dome *e.g. Horse Chestnut*

Narrow or column-like
e.g. silver firs

Conical or pyramidal *e.g. Dawn Redwood, many conifers*

Oval or egg-shaped
e.g. Rowan

Very narrow
e.g. Lombardy Poplar, cypresses

 Coppiced
Branches cut off at ground level

Re-growth after 10 years
e.g. Hazel

 Pollarded
Branches cut off 2-3m above the ground

Re-growth after 10 years
e.g. willows

Trunks

Buttressed
e.g. Western Red Cedar

Fluted
e.g. False Acacia

Gnarled
e.g. Olive

Stout, broad
e.g. English Oak

Long, straight
e.g. pines

Tapering
e.g. Noble Fir

Burrs and bosses *e.g. Black Poplar*

Side-shoots
e.g. Common Lime

Suckers
e.g. Grey Poplar

Divided
e.g. Lilac

Bark Characteristics

Many species of trees have very distinctive bark which can be useful for identifying them, particularly in winter. Bark characteristics to consider when identifying trees include colour, smoothness and pattern of ridging. Young trees usually have fairly smooth bark which becomes more deeply cracked, wrinkled or peeling as the tree matures. The colour of the bark may be hidden by lichen growing on it, or — on town and roadside trees — by a covering of dirt and grime which it will be necessary to scrape away to discover the natural colour.

Illustrated below are examples of the more distinctive barks, showing some of the major characteristics to look for.

Smooth
e.g. Beech

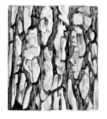

Peeling in plates
e.g. planes

Peeling in strips
e.g . birches

Spirally fissured
e.g. Sweet Chestnut

Spongy and fibrous
e.g. Wellingtonia

Cracked into plates
e.g. pines

Resin blisters
e.g. silver firs

Network of ridges
e.g. willows

Diamond-shaped pits
e.g. White Poplar

Metallic and peeling
e.g. cherries

Very deeply furrowed
e.g. Black Poplar

Corky
e.g. Cork Oak

Flowers and Fruits

All trees bear flowers, but the kind of flower varies considerably from species to species. Types of flowers include the catkins of willows, the tiny petal-less oak flowers, the blossom of fruit trees and the rather insignificant conifer flowers, technically called 'strobili'. Fruits and seeds also show great variation, including nuts, berries, large fleshy fruits, acorns, pods and tiny cottony seeds.

The conifers bear their seeds in cones. Illustrated below are a selection of cones. With practice, it is possible to recognise the different types of cones and the group of conifers to which they belong.

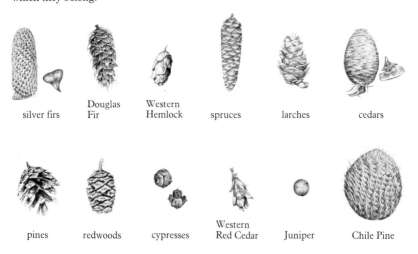

| silver firs | Douglas Fir | Western Hemlock | spruces | larches | cedars |

| pines | redwoods | cypresses | Western Red Cedar | Juniper | Chile Pine |

Seasonal Variations in Trees

All trees vary with the seasons. This is most apparent in deciduous trees, which lose their leaves in winter; but even evergreen trees show quite marked seasonal changes.

Trees spend the winter in a dormant state. The twigs of deciduous trees are bare except for resting winter buds. Evergreen trees retain their leaves but do not grow during these cold months.

With the warmth of spring, buds on both deciduous and evergreen trees burst into new leaves. Twigs elongate with new, green growth. The new leaves are a bright, fresh green — this is especially noticeable on evergreens where they contrast with the dark green old leaves.

In spring or summer, flowers are produced, either before the leaves (as in Ash and Blackthorn) or after the leaves have expanded. Flowers are pollinated, by the wind or by insects, and begin to develop into fruits or cones.

By midsummer, most growth has stopped, next winter's resting buds have been formed and the new twig growth has become hard and woody.

In autumn, fruits and seeds are dispersed, by the wind, by water or by animals, ready to grow into seedlings the following spring. The leaves of deciduous trees die and fall, leaving 'leaf scars' where their stalks have broken from the twig. Evergreen leaves last for several seasons but each year some leaves die and fall from the tree.

Autumn becomes winter and the cycle starts again.

Seasonal Changes in Beech

=WINTER=

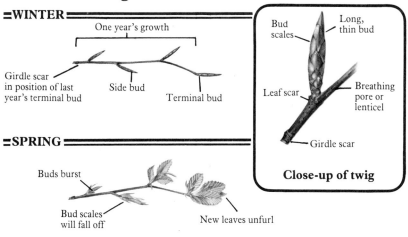

One year's growth

Girdle scar
in position of last
year's terminal bud

Side bud

Terminal bud

Bud
scales

Long,
thin bud

Leaf scar

Breathing
pore or
lenticel

Girdle scar

Close-up of twig

=SPRING=

Buds burst

Bud scales
will fall off

New leaves unfurl

=LATE SPRING=

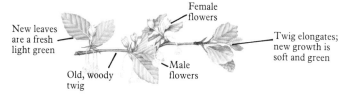

Female
flowers

New leaves
are a fresh
light green

Twig elongates;
new growth is
soft and green

Old, woody
twig

Male
flowers

=SUMMER=

Mature
leaves

New terminal bud

Next winter's resting
buds have formed
in the leaf axils

Female flowers
develop into fruits

=AUTUMN=

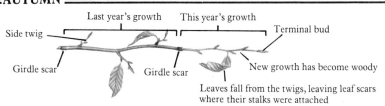

Last year's growth

This year's growth

Side twig

Terminal bud

Girdle scar

Girdle scar

New growth has become woody

Leaves fall from the twigs, leaving leaf scars
where their stalks were attached

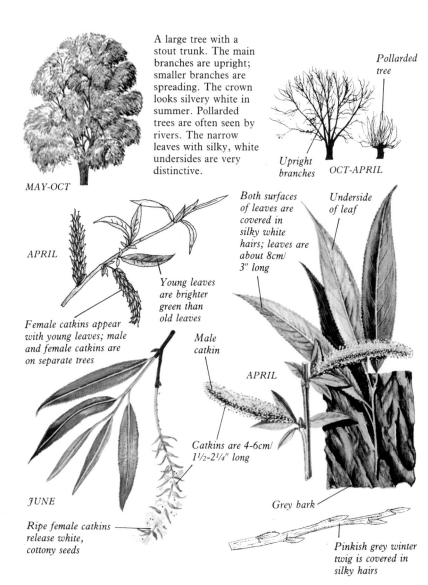

A large tree with a stout trunk. The main branches are upright; smaller branches are spreading. The crown looks silvery white in summer. Pollarded trees are often seen by rivers. The narrow leaves with silky, white undersides are very distinctive.

Pollarded tree

MAY-OCT

Upright branches

OCT-APRIL

APRIL

Female catkins appear with young leaves; male and female catkins are on separate trees

Young leaves are brighter green than old leaves

Both surfaces of leaves are covered in silky white hairs; leaves are about 8cm/ 3" long

Underside of leaf

Male catkin

APRIL

Catkins are 4-6cm/ 1½-2¼" long

JUNE

Ripe female catkins release white, cottony seeds

Grey bark

Pinkish grey winter twig is covered in silky hairs

White Willow

Salix alba   25m/82'

Habitat: Native. Grows by streams and rivers and in wet woods, marshes and fens.

Distribution: Common throughout the British Isles but absent from Shetland.

Similar species: Crack Willow *S. fragilis* (p12): leaves differ. *S. alba x fragilis* and other *Salix* hybrids are very common but are difficult to identify.

OCT-APRIL

A distinctively shaped tree with a broad crown and long, hanging branches which often reach the ground. The long, narrow leaves and weeping habit make this an easy tree to recognise in any season.

MAY-OCT

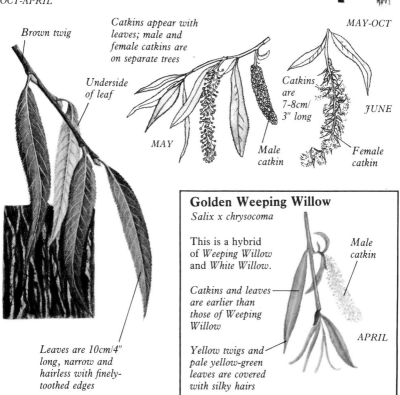

Brown twig

Catkins appear with leaves; male and female catkins are on separate trees

Underside of leaf

Catkins are 7-8cm/ 3" long

JUNE

MAY

Male catkin

Female catkin

Leaves are 10cm/4" long, narrow and hairless with finely-toothed edges

Golden Weeping Willow
Salix x chrysocoma

This is a hybrid of *Weeping Willow* and *White Willow*.

Male catkin

Catkins and leaves are earlier than those of Weeping Willow

APRIL

Yellow twigs and pale yellow-green leaves are covered with silky hairs

Weeping Willow

Salix babylonica   20m/66'
Habitat: Introduced from China. Planted in parks and gardens, often by water.
Distribution: Most common in the southern half of the British Isles.
Similar species: Hybrids of White Willow *S. alba* or Crack Willow *S. fragilis* with Weeping Willow: tree shape usually differs.

11

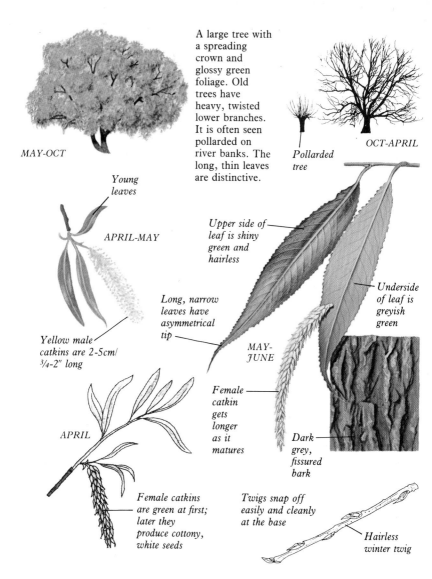

A large tree with a spreading crown and glossy green foliage. Old trees have heavy, twisted lower branches. It is often seen pollarded on river banks. The long, thin leaves are distinctive.

MAY-OCT

OCT-APRIL

Pollarded tree

Young leaves

APRIL-MAY

Upper side of leaf is shiny green and hairless

Underside of leaf is greyish green

Long, narrow leaves have asymmetrical tip

Yellow male catkins are 2-5cm/ ³/₄-2" long

MAY-JUNE

Female catkin gets longer as it matures

Dark grey, fissured bark

APRIL

Female catkins are green at first; later they produce cottony, white seeds

Twigs snap off easily and cleanly at the base

Hairless winter twig

Crack Willow

Salix fragilis   25m/82'
Habitat: Native. Grows by rivers and streams and in wet woodland. Will grow on poorer soils than White Willow. Thrives best in open situations.
Distribution: Common. Native south of Perth. Planted north of Perth and in Ireland.
Similar species: White Willow *S. alba* (p10) and hybrids with other *Salix* spp.

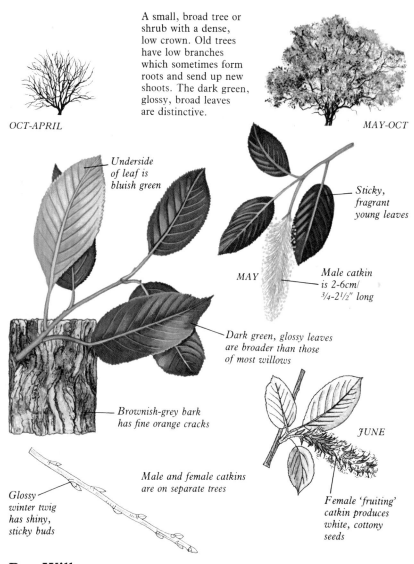

A small, broad tree or shrub with a dense, low crown. Old trees have low branches which sometimes form roots and send up new shoots. The dark green, glossy, broad leaves are distinctive.

OCT-APRIL

MAY-OCT

Underside of leaf is bluish green

Sticky, fragrant young leaves

MAY

Male catkin is 2-6cm/ ³/₄-2¹/₂" long

Dark green, glossy leaves are broader than those of most willows

Brownish-grey bark has fine orange cracks

JUNE

Male and female catkins are on separate trees

Glossy winter twig has shiny, sticky buds

Female 'fruiting' catkin produces white, cottony seeds

Bay Willow

Salix pentandra 7m/23'

Habitat: Native. Grows in marshes, fens, wet woods and by streams. Rarely planted.

Distribution: Common in N. Wales, N. England, Scotland and N. Ireland; uncommon in S. England, S. Wales and S. Ireland.

Similar species: Other willows (*Salix* spp): leaf shapes and colour differ.

13

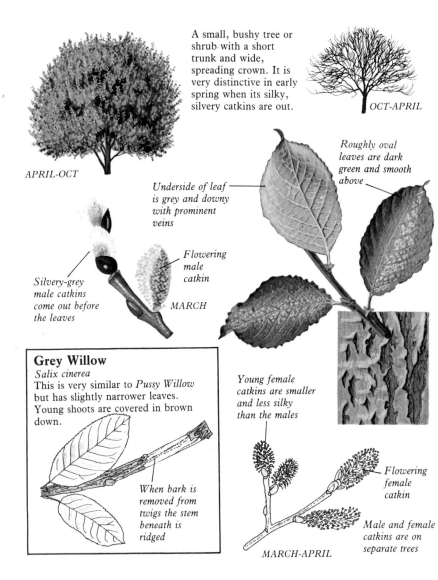

A small, bushy tree or shrub with a short trunk and wide, spreading crown. It is very distinctive in early spring when its silky, silvery catkins are out.

OCT-APRIL

APRIL-OCT

Underside of leaf is grey and downy with prominent veins

Roughly oval leaves are dark green and smooth above

Flowering male catkin

MARCH

Silvery-grey male catkins come out before the leaves

Grey Willow
Salix cinerea
This is very similar to *Pussy Willow* but has slightly narrower leaves. Young shoots are covered in brown down.

When bark is removed from twigs the stem beneath is ridged

Young female catkins are smaller and less silky than the males

Flowering female catkin

Male and female catkins are on separate trees

MARCH-APRIL

Goat or Pussy Willow

Salix caprea   10m/33'
Habitat: Native. Grows in woodland, hedgerows and scrub. It will tolerate wet, exposed or shady sites. (Grey Willow *S. cinerea* is found on more moist sites.)
Distribution: Common throughout the British Isles and to over 700m/2300' in Scotland.
Similar species: Grey Willow *S. cinerea* (see above).

14

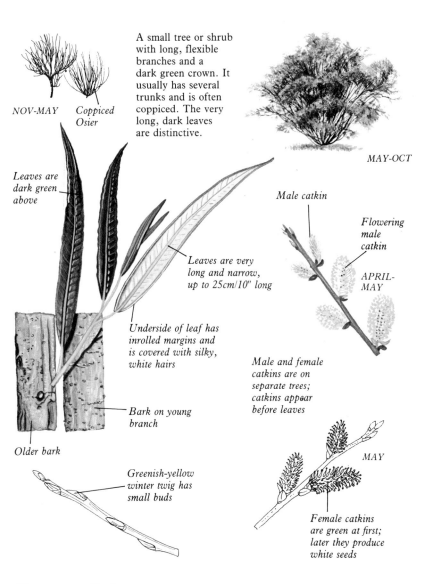

NOV-MAY — *Coppiced Osier*

A small tree or shrub with long, flexible branches and a dark green crown. It usually has several trunks and is often coppiced. The very long, dark leaves are distinctive.

MAY-OCT

Leaves are dark green above

Male catkin

Flowering male catkin

APRIL-MAY

Leaves are very long and narrow, up to 25cm/10" long

Underside of leaf has inrolled margins and is covered with silky, white hairs

Male and female catkins are on separate trees; catkins appear before leaves

Older bark

Bark on young branch

Greenish-yellow winter twig has small buds

MAY

Female catkins are green at first; later they produce white seeds

Common Osier

Salix viminalis   5m/16'
Habitat: Native. Grows by ponds and streams and in fens, usually on moist soils.
Distribution: Frequent throughout lowland areas of the British Isles.
Similar species: Hybrids of *S. viminalis* with other *Salix* spp. Purple Osier *S. purpurea*, also coppiced for basket-making, has shorter leaves and hairless buds.

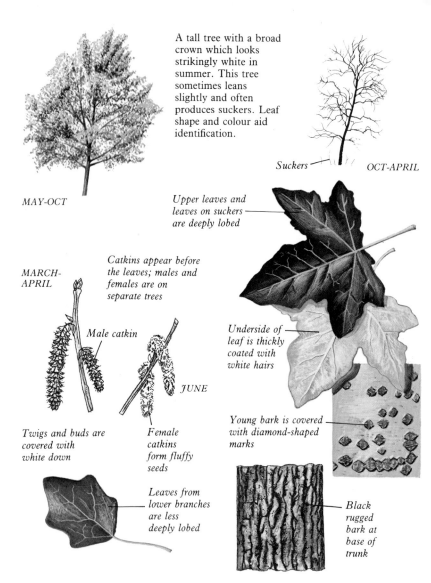

A tall tree with a broad crown which looks strikingly white in summer. This tree sometimes leans slightly and often produces suckers. Leaf shape and colour aid identification.

Suckers — OCT-APRIL

MAY-OCT

Upper leaves and leaves on suckers are deeply lobed

MARCH-APRIL

Catkins appear before the leaves; males and females are on separate trees

Male catkin

JUNE

Underside of leaf is thickly coated with white hairs

Twigs and buds are covered with white down

Female catkins form fluffy seeds

Young bark is covered with diamond-shaped marks

Leaves from lower branches are less deeply lobed

Black rugged bark at base of trunk

White Poplar or Abele

Populus alba   20m/66'
Habitat: Early introduction from Europe. Planted in parks, along roadsides and in sandy, coastal areas. Sometimes naturalized in woods.
Distribution: Common throughout the British Isles.
Similar species: Grey Poplar *P. canescens* (p17): leaf shape differs.

16

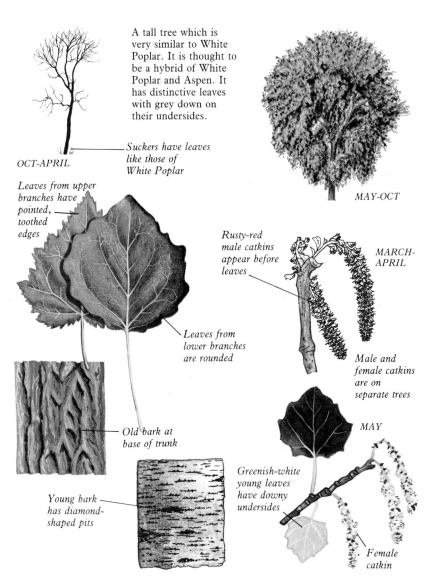

A tall tree which is very similar to White Poplar. It is thought to be a hybrid of White Poplar and Aspen. It has distinctive leaves with grey down on their undersides.

OCT-APRIL

Suckers have leaves like those of White Poplar

MAY-OCT

Leaves from upper branches have pointed, toothed edges

Rusty-red male catkins appear before leaves

MARCH-APRIL

Leaves from lower branches are rounded

Male and female catkins are on separate trees

MAY

Old bark at base of trunk

Greenish-white young leaves have downy undersides

Young bark has diamond-shaped pits

Female catkin

Grey Poplar

Populus canescens 35m/115'
Habitat: Probably introduced from Europe. Grows in damp woods. Planted by roads.
Distribution: Locally abundant. Naturalized in S. England, planted elsewhere.
Similar species: White Poplar *P. alba* (p16) and Aspen *P. tremula* (p18): leaf shape and undersides of leaves differ.

17

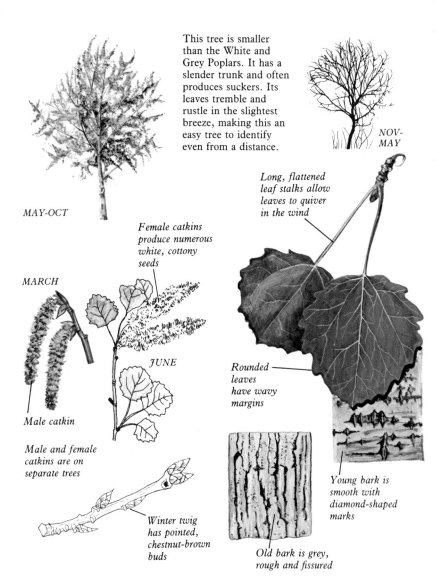

This tree is smaller than the White and Grey Poplars. It has a slender trunk and often produces suckers. Its leaves tremble and rustle in the slightest breeze, making this an easy tree to identify even from a distance.

NOV-MAY

MAY-OCT

Long, flattened leaf stalks allow leaves to quiver in the wind

Female catkins produce numerous white, cottony seeds

MARCH

JUNE

Rounded leaves have wavy margins

Male catkin

Male and female catkins are on separate trees

Winter twig has pointed, chestnut-brown buds

Young bark is smooth with diamond-shaped marks

Old bark is grey, rough and fissured

Aspen

Populus tremula   20m/66'
Habitat: Native. Grows in woods on poorer soils and in damp, upland areas.
Distribution: Common throughout the British Isles.
Similar species: Grey Poplar *P. canescens* (p17) has a less rounded leaf with grey down beneath and lacks Aspen's long, flattened leaf stalk.

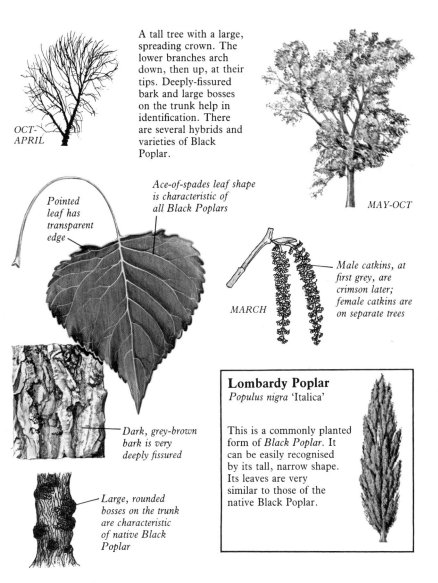

A tall tree with a large, spreading crown. The lower branches arch down, then up, at their tips. Deeply-fissured bark and large bosses on the trunk help in identification. There are several hybrids and varieties of Black Poplar.

OCT-APRIL

MAY-OCT

Ace-of-spades leaf shape is characteristic of all Black Poplars

Pointed leaf has transparent edge

MARCH

Male catkins, at first grey, are crimson later; female catkins are on separate trees

Dark, grey-brown bark is very deeply fissured

Large, rounded bosses on the trunk are characteristic of native Black Poplar

Lombardy Poplar
Populus nigra 'Italica'

This is a commonly planted form of *Black Poplar*. It can be easily recognised by its tall, narrow shape. Its leaves are very similar to those of the native Black Poplar.

Black Poplar

Populus nigra   30m/100'
Habitat: Native. Grows by rivers and in damp woods and hedgerows.
Distribution: Uncommon in southern and central England; rare elsewhere.
Similar species: Hybrids of Black Poplar, especially *P. x canadensis:* this tree has ascending branches and is always male. Hybrids are commonly planted.

19

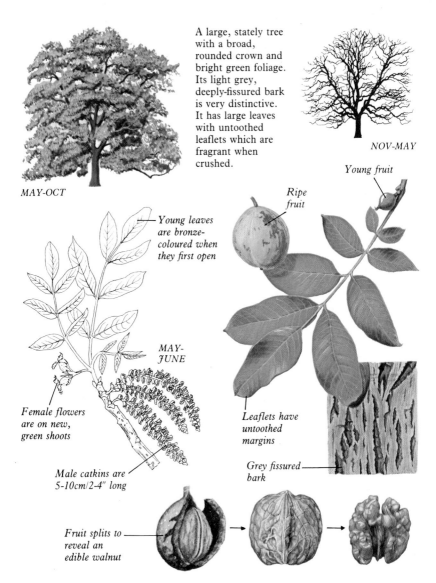

A large, stately tree with a broad, rounded crown and bright green foliage. Its light grey, deeply-fissured bark is very distinctive. It has large leaves with untoothed leaflets which are fragrant when crushed.

MAY-OCT

NOV-MAY

Young fruit

Ripe fruit

Young leaves are bronze-coloured when they first open

MAY-JUNE

Female flowers are on new, green shoots

Male catkins are 5-10cm/2-4" long

Leaflets have untoothed margins

Grey fissured bark

Fruit splits to reveal an edible walnut

Common Walnut

Juglans regia   30m/100'

Habitat: Introduced from S.E. Europe. Planted in parks and gardens on any soil.
Distribution: Common in S. England; uncommon in the rest of the British Isles.
Similar species: Other walnuts (*Juglans* spp): serrated leaflets distinguish them.

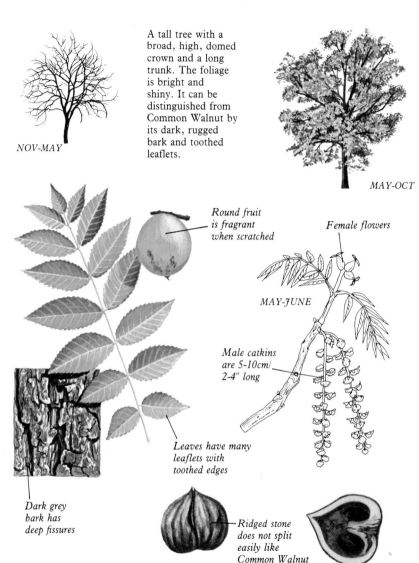

A tall tree with a broad, high, domed crown and a long trunk. The foliage is bright and shiny. It can be distinguished from Common Walnut by its dark, rugged bark and toothed leaflets.

NOV-MAY

MAY-OCT

Round fruit is fragrant when scratched

Female flowers

MAY-JUNE

Male catkins are 5-10cm/ 2-4" long

Leaves have many leaflets with toothed edges

Dark grey bark has deep fissures

Ridged stone does not split easily like Common Walnut

Black Walnut

Juglans nigra   30m/100'
Habitat: Introduced from North America. Planted in parks and gardens. Grows best in rich, damp soils, in sheltered, warm positions.
Distribution: Uncommon in S. England; rare in Scotland and Ireland.
Similar species: Butternut *J. cinerea* has hairier leaves and pointed fruits.

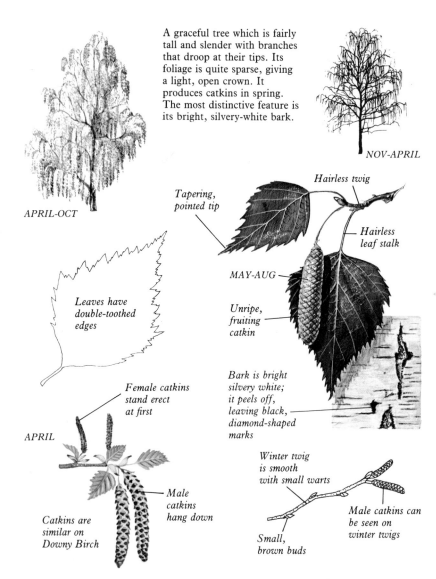

A graceful tree which is fairly tall and slender with branches that droop at their tips. Its foliage is quite sparse, giving a light, open crown. It produces catkins in spring. The most distinctive feature is its bright, silvery-white bark.

NOV-APRIL

APRIL-OCT

Tapering, pointed tip

Hairless twig

Hairless leaf stalk

MAY-AUG

Leaves have double-toothed edges

Unripe, fruiting catkin

Bark is bright silvery white; it peels off, leaving black, diamond-shaped marks

Female catkins stand erect at first

APRIL

Male catkins hang down

Catkins are similar on Downy Birch

Winter twig is smooth with small warts

Male catkins can be seen on winter twigs

Small, brown buds

Silver Birch

Betula pendula   25m/82'
Habitat: Native. Grows on light soils, rarely on chalk, in drier situations than Downy Birch. Found in woods, scrub, on heathland, moors and hills.
Distribution: Common throughout the British Isles, especially in the South and East.
Similar species: Downy Birch *B. pubescens* (p23): tree shape and leaves differ.

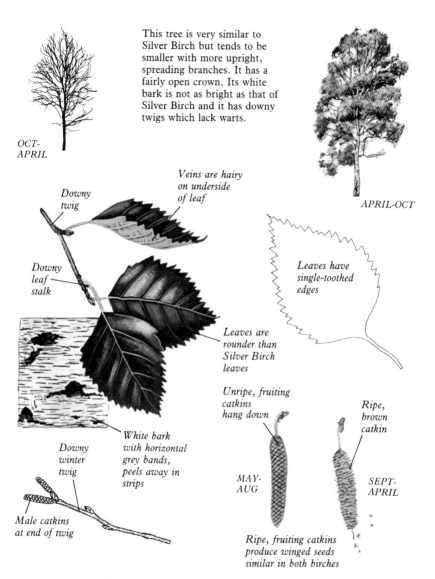

This tree is very similar to Silver Birch but tends to be smaller with more upright, spreading branches. It has a fairly open crown. Its white bark is not as bright as that of Silver Birch and it has downy twigs which lack warts.

OCT-APRIL

APRIL-OCT

Veins are hairy on underside of leaf

Downy twig

Downy leaf stalk

Leaves have single-toothed edges

Leaves are rounder than Silver Birch leaves

White bark with horizontal grey bands, peels away in strips

Downy winter twig

Male catkins at end of twig

Unripe, fruiting catkins hang down

Ripe, brown catkin

MAY-AUG

SEPT-APRIL

Ripe, fruiting catkins produce winged seeds similar in both birches

Downy Birch

Betula pubescens   20m/66'

Habitat: Native. Grows on heaths, moors and in woods on light soils. It is more tolerant of cold and wet upland conditions than Silver Birch.

Distribution: Frequent throughout the British Isles; common in the North and West.

Similar species: Silver Birch *B. pendula* (p22): tree shape and leaves differ.

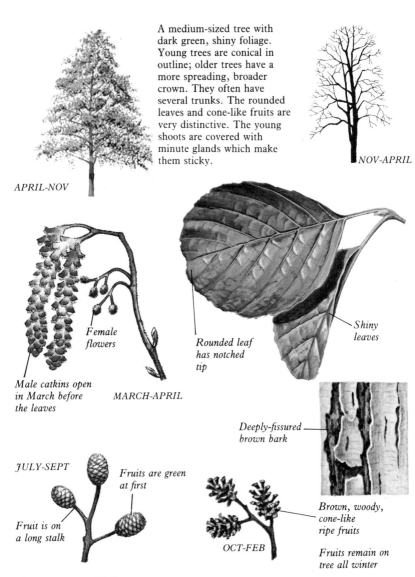

A medium-sized tree with dark green, shiny foliage. Young trees are conical in outline; older trees have a more spreading, broader crown. They often have several trunks. The rounded leaves and cone-like fruits are very distinctive. The young shoots are covered with minute glands which make them sticky.

APRIL-NOV

NOV-APRIL

Female flowers

Rounded leaf has notched tip

Shiny leaves

Male catkins open in March before the leaves

MARCH-APRIL

Deeply-fissured brown bark

JULY-SEPT

Fruits are green at first

Fruit is on a long stalk

OCT-FEB

Brown, woody, cone-like ripe fruits

Fruits remain on tree all winter

Common Alder

Alnus glutinosa   25m/82'
Habitat: Native. Grows on wet soils by rivers, forming woods in marshy areas.
Distribution: Common throughout the British Isles.
Similar species: Italian Alder *A. cordata* has dark, pointed, shiny leaves bearing tufts of orange hairs beneath and is planted in streets.

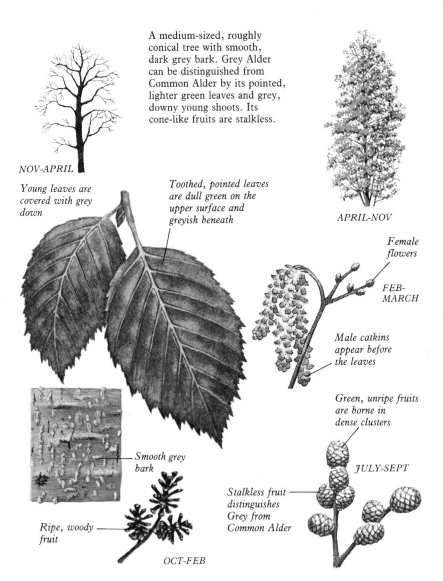

A medium-sized, roughly conical tree with smooth, dark grey bark. Grey Alder can be distinguished from Common Alder by its pointed, lighter green leaves and grey, downy young shoots. Its cone-like fruits are stalkless.

NOV-APRIL

Young leaves are covered with grey down

Toothed, pointed leaves are dull green on the upper surface and greyish beneath

APRIL-NOV

Female flowers

FEB-MARCH

Male catkins appear before the leaves

Green, unripe fruits are borne in dense clusters

JULY-SEPT

Smooth grey bark

Stalkless fruit distinguishes Grey from Common Alder

Ripe, woody fruit

OCT-FEB

Grey Alder

Alnus incana   20m/66'
Habitat: Introduced from Europe. Often planted on poor or wet soils and on reclaimed land, such as disused quarries. It will tolerate wet conditions.
Distribution: Locally abundant throughout the British Isles.
Similar species: Other alders (*Alnus* spp): they lack grey, downy young shoots.

25

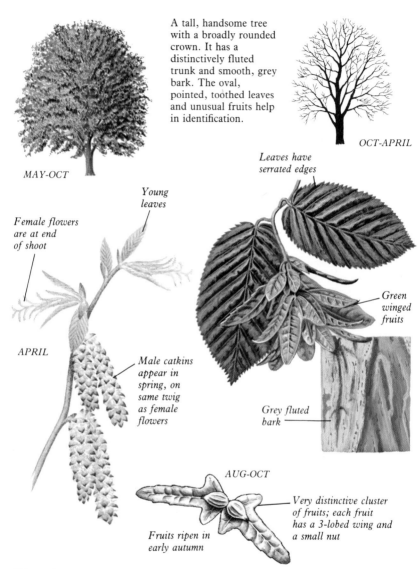

A tall, handsome tree with a broadly rounded crown. It has a distinctively fluted trunk and smooth, grey bark. The oval, pointed, toothed leaves and unusual fruits help in identification.

OCT-APRIL

MAY-OCT

Leaves have serrated edges

Young leaves

Female flowers are at end of shoot

Green winged fruits

APRIL

Male catkins appear in spring, on same twig as female flowers

Grey fluted bark

AUG-OCT

Very distinctive cluster of fruits; each fruit has a 3-lobed wing and a small nut

Fruits ripen in early autumn

Hornbeam

Carpinus betulus   25m/82'
Habitat: Native. Grows in woods and hedgerows in S. England. Also planted as a hedge.
Distribution: Common in S. England; frequently planted elsewhere.
Similar species: Beech *Fagus sylvatica* (p30) has leaves with untoothed margins. Raoul *Nothofagus procera* (p29) has leaves with wavy or slightly serrated margins.

OCT-APRIL

This tree is similar to Hornbeam although it is usually smaller. Young trees have narrow, conical crowns; older trees are broad-crowned. It has a short, stout trunk with brownish-grey bark. The hop-like fruits are distinctive.

MAY-OCT

Leaves are similar to Hornbeam leaves

Hairy young leaves

NOV-FEB

APRIL

Male catkins elongate and produce pollen in spring

Male catkins are at end of twig in winter

Fissured bark

AUG

Clusters of whitish-green hop-like fruits turn brown in autumn

Single fruit

Each fruit is a small nut in a papery, bladder-like husk

European Hop-hornbeam

Ostrya carpinifolia 20m/66'

Habitat: Introduced from S. Europe. Grown here in parks and gardens, on any soil.

Distribution: Rare. Found only in larger tree collections.

Similar species: Hornbeam *Carpinus betulus* (p26) has similar leaves but quite different fruit and its male catkins are not visible in winter.

27

A small shrub or tree, usually with several stems. It sometimes forms dense thickets. Hazel is often coppiced in woodlands. The nuts are distinctive and its toothed, downy leaves aid identification.

DEC-APRIL

MAY-NOV

Downy twig

Broad, rounded leaves have toothed edges

FEB-MARCH

Long male catkins shed pollen in February, before the leaves come out

Female flowers have red tufts

Leaf is downy on both sides; young leaf feels soft

Nut

Fruit (hazelnut) is held in a green husk with toothed edges

Ripe brown nuts contain edible kernels

Kernel

AUG-SEPT

Nut

SEPT

Hazel

Corylus avellana   6m/20'

Habitat: Native. Grows in woods and hedgerows; often forms the shrub layer in woods. Grows on chalk, limestone, neutral or moderately acidic soils.

Distribution: Common throughout the British Isles except Shetland.

Similar species: Filbert *C. maxima* has nuts enclosed in a long tube of bracts.

A conical tree with dense foliage. The branches are arranged around the trunk in rings or whorls. It has narrow, oval leaves with prominent veins and distinctive prickly fruits.

OCT-APRIL

MAY-OCT

Leaves have prominent pairs of veins; veins on underside have silky hairs

Dark brown, rough shoots have small warts

Unripe fruits

JULY-AUG

MAY

Flowers

Smooth, grey-brown bark with wide, dark cracks

Prickly ripe fruit

Scales

Hairy winter twig has pointed, angled buds

Each fruit contains 3 nuts; the centre nut is flattened

SEPT-OCT

Raoul or Rauli

Nothofagus procera   25m/82′

Habitat: Introduced from Chile. Planted in large gardens and in a few plantations.

Distribution: Uncommon. Slightly more frequent in Wales and W. England.

Similar species: Hornbeam (p26). Common Beech (p30). Roble Beech *N. obliqua* has fewer veins on its leaves (8-11 pairs of veins as opposed to Raoul's 14-18 pairs).

29

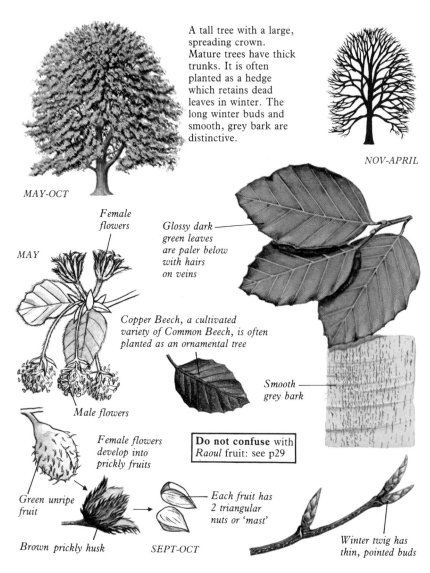

A tall tree with a large, spreading crown. Mature trees have thick trunks. It is often planted as a hedge which retains dead leaves in winter. The long winter buds and smooth, grey bark are distinctive.

NOV-APRIL

MAY-OCT

Female flowers

MAY

Glossy dark green leaves are paler below with hairs on veins

Copper Beech, a cultivated variety of Common Beech, is often planted as an ornamental tree

Smooth grey bark

Male flowers

Female flowers develop into prickly fruits

Do not confuse with *Raoul* fruit: see p29

Green unripe fruit

Each fruit has 2 triangular nuts or 'mast'

Brown prickly husk   *SEPT-OCT*

Winter twig has thin, pointed buds

Common Beech

Fagus sylvatica   30m/100'
Habitat: Native to S.E. England. It forms large woods on chalk and limestone hills, growing best on a well-drained soil. It is often planted in parks and gardens.
Distribution: Common throughout the British Isles.
Similar species: Hornbeam (p26) and Raoul (p29): bark, leaves and fruit differ.

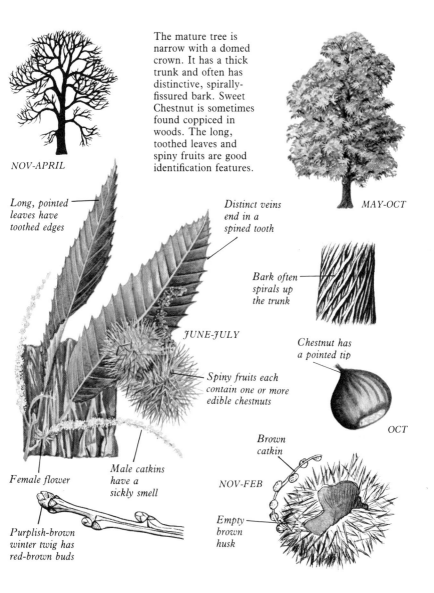

The mature tree is narrow with a domed crown. It has a thick trunk and often has distinctive, spirally-fissured bark. Sweet Chestnut is sometimes found coppiced in woods. The long, toothed leaves and spiny fruits are good identification features.

NOV-APRIL

MAY-OCT

Long, pointed leaves have toothed edges

Distinct veins end in a spined tooth

Bark often spirals up the trunk

JUNE-JULY

Chestnut has a pointed tip

Spiny fruits each contain one or more edible chestnuts

OCT

Female flower

Male catkins have a sickly smell

Brown catkin

NOV-FEB

Purplish-brown winter twig has red-brown buds

Empty brown husk

Sweet Chestnut

Castanea sativa   30m/100'
Habitat: Introduced from S. Europe. Grows best on light, well-drained, acid or neutral soils. Planted in parks and naturalized (often coppiced) in woods.
Distribution: Common in the southern half of Britain; frequent elsewhere.

31

The mature tree has a stout trunk with spreading, twisted branches, forming a broad, rounded crown. This tree is often wider than its height. Its acorns are on long stalks.

NOV-APRIL

MAY-OCT

Reddish-green young leaves

Leaves have deep, rounded lobes with 2 small lobes or 'auricles' at the leaf base

APRIL

Young acorns are green, turning brown by October

Female flowers are on end of new shoot

Auricle

Slender male catkins

Acorns are on long stalks; leaves are stalkless

Pale, grey-brown bark

Brown, woody oak apples are produced by gall wasps on some trees

Grey-brown winter twig has light-brown buds

Empty acorn cups

NOV-MARCH

Cluster of buds

English or Pedunculate Oak

Quercus robur   45m/150′
Habitat: Native. It is usually the dominant woodland tree especially on non-acid clays and loams. It has been very widely planted in hedgerows, parks and large gardens.
Distribution: Common throughout the British Isles.
Similar species: Sessile Oak (p33). Hybrids of English and Sessile Oaks are common.

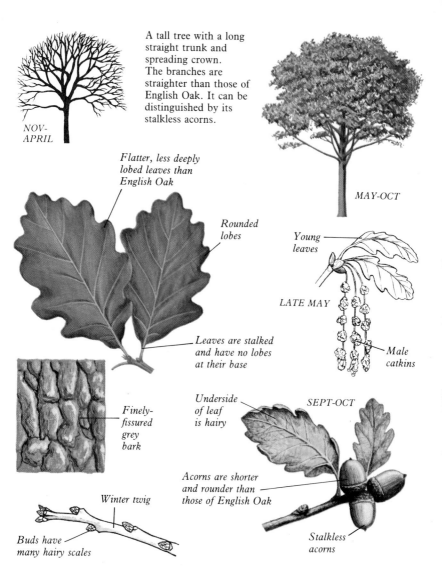

A tall tree with a long straight trunk and spreading crown. The branches are straighter than those of English Oak. It can be distinguished by its stalkless acorns.

NOV-APRIL

MAY-OCT

Flatter, less deeply lobed leaves than English Oak

Rounded lobes

Young leaves

LATE MAY

Male catkins

Leaves are stalked and have no lobes at their base

Finely-fissured grey bark

Underside of leaf is hairy

SEPT-OCT

Acorns are shorter and rounder than those of English Oak

Winter twig

Buds have many hairy scales

Stalkless acorns

Sessile or Durmast Oak

Quercus petraea   40m/130'

Habitat: Native. Grows in woods, sometimes with English Oak. Grows well on acidic soils; tolerates flooded or well-drained soils.

Distribution: Common in the hills of N.W. Britain; frequent elsewhere.

Similar species: English Oak (p32). White Oak *Q. pubescens* has hairy leaf stalks.

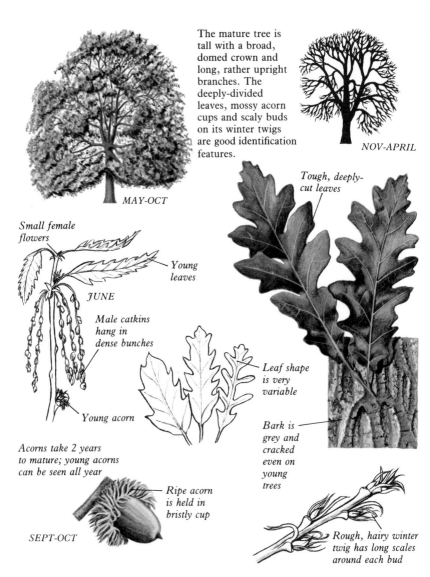

The mature tree is tall with a broad, domed crown and long, rather upright branches. The deeply-divided leaves, mossy acorn cups and scaly buds on its winter twigs are good identification features.

MAY-OCT

NOV-APRIL

Tough, deeply-cut leaves

Small female flowers

Young leaves

JUNE

Male catkins hang in dense bunches

Leaf shape is very variable

Young acorn

Bark is grey and cracked even on young trees

Acorns take 2 years to mature; young acorns can be seen all year

Ripe acorn is held in bristly cup

SEPT-OCT

Rough, hairy winter twig has long scales around each bud

Turkey Oak

Quercus cerris   35m/115'
Habitat: Introduced from southern and central Europe. Planted in parks and on roadsides and naturalized in woods and hedgerows in S. England.
Distribution: Common throughout the British Isles.
Similar species: Other oaks (*Quercus* spp): they lack mossy acorn cups.

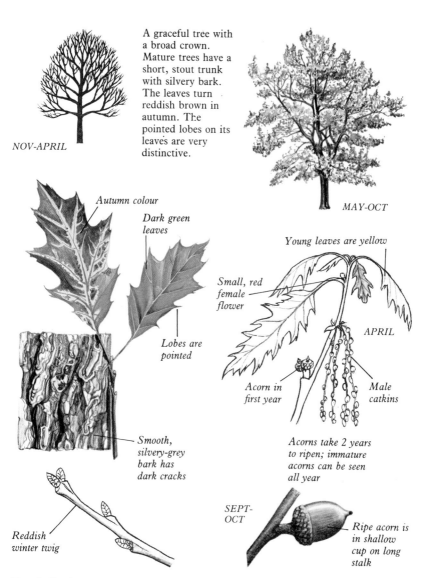

A graceful tree with a broad crown. Mature trees have a short, stout trunk with silvery bark. The leaves turn reddish brown in autumn. The pointed lobes on its leaves are very distinctive.

NOV-APRIL

MAY-OCT

Autumn colour

Dark green leaves

Lobes are pointed

Smooth, silvery-grey bark has dark cracks

Reddish winter twig

Young leaves are yellow

Small, red female flower

APRIL

Acorn in first year

Male catkins

Acorns take 2 years to ripen; immature acorns can be seen all year

SEPT-OCT

Ripe acorn is in shallow cup on long stalk

Red Oak

Quercus borealis   25m/82'
Habitat: Introduced from North America. Planted in parks, gardens and by roads.
Distribution: Frequent throughout the British Isles.
Similar species: Scarlet Oak *Q. coccinea* has similar pointed leaf lobes but they are usually more deeply cut, and its leaves are glossy on both sides.

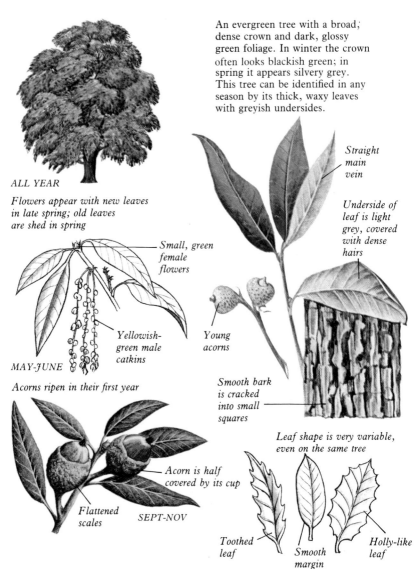

An evergreen tree with a broad, dense crown and dark, glossy green foliage. In winter the crown often looks blackish green; in spring it appears silvery grey. This tree can be identified in any season by its thick, waxy leaves with greyish undersides.

ALL YEAR

Flowers appear with new leaves in late spring; old leaves are shed in spring

Straight main vein

Underside of leaf is light grey, covered with dense hairs

Small, green female flowers

Yellowish-green male catkins

MAY-JUNE

Young acorns

Acorns ripen in their first year

Smooth bark is cracked into small squares

Acorn is half covered by its cup

Flattened scales

SEPT-NOV

Leaf shape is very variable, even on the same tree

Toothed leaf

Smooth margin

Holly-like leaf

Holm Oak

Quercus ilex   25m/82′
Habitat: Introduced from the Mediterranean. Planted in parks and gardens.
Distribution: Common throughout the British Isles, especially in southern, coastal areas.
Similar species: Cork Oak *Q. suber* (p37) has distinctive bark and leaves. Other evergreen oaks can be distinguished by their leaf shape and size.

A spreading evergreen tree with heavy, twisted branches and thick, corky bark. The bark is used commercially for cork production. This tree can be easily identified by its corky bark and holly-like evergreen leaves.

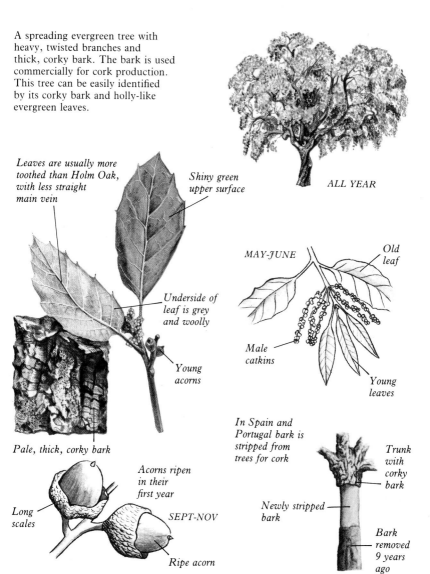

ALL YEAR

Leaves are usually more toothed than Holm Oak, with less straight main vein

Shiny green upper surface

MAY-JUNE

Old leaf

Underside of leaf is grey and woolly

Male catkins

Young leaves

Young acorns

Pale, thick, corky bark

In Spain and Portugal bark is stripped from trees for cork

Trunk with corky bark

Newly stripped bark

Bark removed 9 years ago

Acorns ripen in their first year

Long scales

SEPT-NOV

Ripe acorn

Cork Oak

Quercus suber   20m/66'
Habitat: Introduced from S. Europe. Planted in parks and large gardens.
Distribution: Uncommon. Most frequent in S.W. England.
Similar species: Holm Oak *Q. ilex* (p36) and Spanish Oak *Q. x hispanica* (a hybrid of Cork Oak and Turkey Oak): leaf shape, bark and crown differ.

37

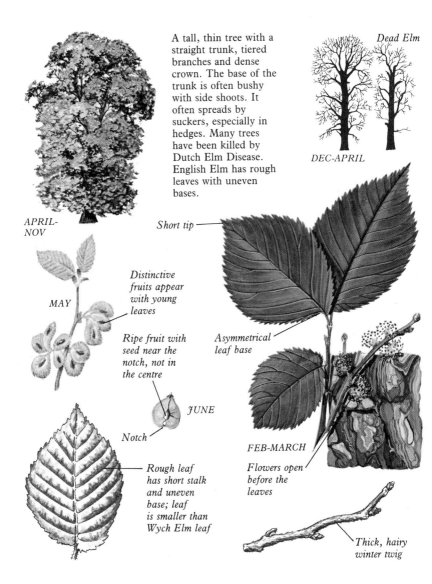

A tall, thin tree with a straight trunk, tiered branches and dense crown. The base of the trunk is often bushy with side shoots. It often spreads by suckers, especially in hedges. Many trees have been killed by Dutch Elm Disease. English Elm has rough leaves with uneven bases.

Dead Elm

DEC-APRIL

APRIL-NOV

Short tip

MAY

Distinctive fruits appear with young leaves

Ripe fruit with seed near the notch, not in the centre

JUNE

Notch

Asymmetrical leaf base

FEB-MARCH

Rough leaf has short stalk and uneven base; leaf is smaller than Wych Elm leaf

Flowers open before the leaves

Thick, hairy winter twig

English Elm

Ulmus procera   30m/100'
Habitat: Native. Grows in hedgerows and by roadsides; seldom in woodlands.
Distribution: Used to be very common in S. England and the Midlands but has now been devastated by Dutch Elm disease. Rare in Scotland, Ireland and E. Anglia.
Similar species: Other elms (*Ulmus* spp): crown shapes differ.

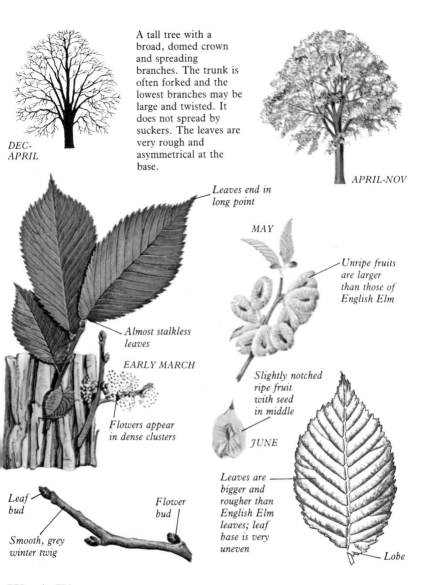

A tall tree with a broad, domed crown and spreading branches. The trunk is often forked and the lowest branches may be large and twisted. It does not spread by suckers. The leaves are very rough and asymmetrical at the base.

DEC-APRIL

APRIL-NOV

Leaves end in long point

MAY

Unripe fruits are larger than those of English Elm

Almost stalkless leaves

EARLY MARCH

Slightly notched ripe fruit with seed in middle

JUNE

Flowers appear in dense clusters

Leaves are bigger and rougher than English Elm leaves; leaf base is very uneven

Leaf bud

Flower bud

Smooth, grey winter twig

Lobe

Wych Elm

Ulmus glabra   40m/130'
Habitat: Native. Grows in woods and hedges, often by water, on moist, deep soils.
Distribution: Common throughout the British Isles but most frequent in Wales, N. England and Scotland.
Similar species: Other elms (*Ulmus* spp). Hybridises with Smooth-leaved Elm (p40).

A tall tree with a fairly narrow crown and many upright branches. It often forms suckers. The leaves open late, making its crown look airy in spring when English Elm is dark green.

DEC-MAY

JUNE-NOV

MAY-JUNE

Fruits are similar to those of other elms

Ripe fruit with seed near notch

MAY

Notch

Flowers

MARCH

Leaf is broadest nearer tip than middle

Smooth, bright green, shiny leaves are narrower than those of other elms

Bark has long, deep cracks

Leaf bud

Round flower bud

Slender, hairless winter twig

Smooth-leaved Elm

Ulmus minor   30m/100'
Habitat: Native. Grows in small woods and hedgerows.
Distribution: Common in S. England and East Anglia; uncommon in the Midlands. Rarely found north or west of the Midlands.
Similar species: Other elms (*Ulmus* spp). Often hybridises with Wych Elm (p39).

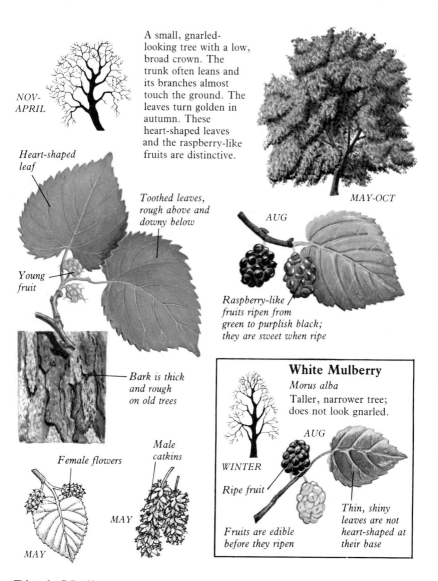

NOV-APRIL

A small, gnarled-looking tree with a low, broad crown. The trunk often leans and its branches almost touch the ground. The leaves turn golden in autumn. These heart-shaped leaves and the raspberry-like fruits are distinctive.

MAY-OCT

Heart-shaped leaf

Toothed leaves, rough above and downy below

AUG

Young fruit

Raspberry-like fruits ripen from green to purplish black; they are sweet when ripe

Bark is thick and rough on old trees

White Mulberry

Morus alba
Taller, narrower tree; does not look gnarled.

WINTER

AUG

Ripe fruit

Fruits are edible before they ripen

Thin, shiny leaves are not heart-shaped at their base

Female flowers

Male catkins

MAY

MAY

MAY

Black Mulberry

Morus nigra   12m/40'
Habitat: Introduced from central Asia. Cultivated in parks and gardens, usually in warm, sunny situations.
Distribution: Frequent in S. England; uncommon elsewhere.
Similar species: White Mulberry *Morus alba* (see above).

An ornamental evergreen tree which is often planted against a wall. As a free-standing tree it has a narrow, conical crown. It is easily identified in any season by its large, glossy, evergreen leaves. In summer and autumn its fragrant white flowers are distinctive.

Planted against a wall

ALL YEAR

Large, white fragrant flower

Leaves often have wavy edges

AUG-NOV

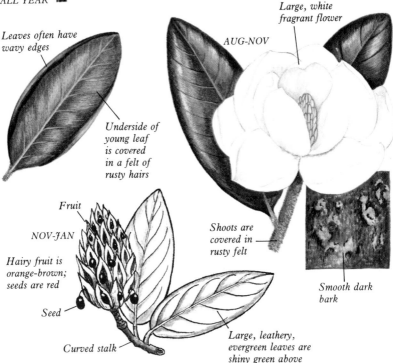

Underside of young leaf is covered in a felt of rusty hairs

Fruit

NOV-JAN

Shoots are covered in rusty felt

Hairy fruit is orange-brown; seeds are red

Seed

Smooth dark bark

Curved stalk

Large, leathery, evergreen leaves are shiny green above

Evergreen Magnolia or Bull Bay

Magnolia grandiflora   10m/33'

Habitat: Introduced from S.E. United States of America. Grown in gardens and town parks, usually in a warm, sunny position against a wall.

Distribution: Common in S. England and Ireland; rare in the rest of the British Isles.

Similar species: Other *Magnolia* spp: they have deciduous, not evergreen leaves.

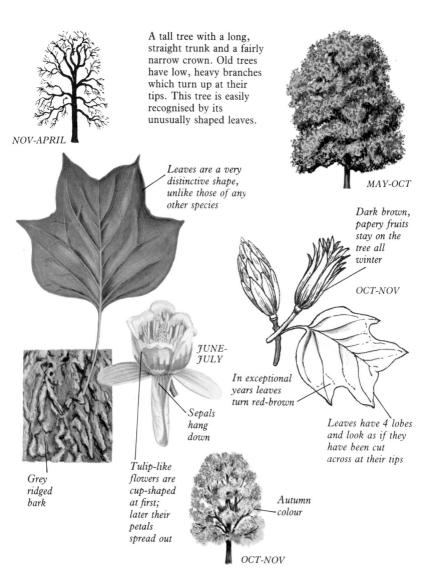

A tall tree with a long, straight trunk and a fairly narrow crown. Old trees have low, heavy branches which turn up at their tips. This tree is easily recognised by its unusually shaped leaves.

NOV-APRIL

MAY-OCT

Leaves are a very distinctive shape, unlike those of any other species

Dark brown, papery fruits stay on the tree all winter

OCT-NOV

JUNE-JULY

In exceptional years leaves turn red-brown

Sepals hang down

Leaves have 4 lobes and look as if they have been cut across at their tips

Grey ridged bark

Tulip-like flowers are cup-shaped at first; later their petals spread out

Autumn colour

OCT-NOV

Tulip Tree

Liriodendron tulipifera   10m/33'
Habitat: Introduced from eastern North America. Grown in parks and gardens.
Distribution: Common in S. England and the Midlands; uncommon in Wales, Ireland and S. Scotland; rare elsewhere.
Similar species: Oriental Tulip Tree *L. chinense* has smaller leaves.

An evergreen tree or shrub with a dense, conical crown and dark green foliage. It is often seen growing in tubs. It can be recognised by its crinkly-edged leaves which are very aromatic when crushed and are used in cooking.

Clipped Bay

ALL YEAR

Dull, paler green underside of leaf has distinctive pattern

Crinkled leaf edge

Pale, yellowish-green male and female flowers are on different trees

JUNE

Dark green, leathery leaves are shiny above

Male flowers

Red leaf stalk

Female flowers

Ripe berries

SEPT

Smooth bark

AUG

Fruits are shiny and green in summer, turning black when ripe

Unripe fruits

Sweet Bay or Bay Laurel

Laurus nobilis   15m/50′
Habitat: Introduced. Planted as an ornamental tree or shrub, often in tubs.
Distribution: Frequent in S. England and Ireland; rare elsewhere.
Similar species: Portugal Laurel (p64), Cherry Laurel (p65) and Strawberry Tree (p85): fruits and flowers differ and they have non-fragrant leaves.

44

A small evergreen tree or shrub with dense, glossy foliage. It often has more than one trunk and is commonly leaning or lop-sided. It is more usually seen as a shrub or clipped hedge. It can be recognised by its small, oval leaves and distinctive fruits.

Box topiary

ALL YEAR

Dark green, glossy, leathery leaves are in opposite pairs

Clusters of yellowish flowers are at the base of leaves; usually a female flower is surrounded by males

Paler underside

Notched leaf tip

Square, hairy stem

APRIL

Brownish-grey bark is deeply cut into small squares

SEPT

Seeds

Ripe fruit

Fruit is a 3-horned, papery capsule which opens suddenly, releasing small, black seeds

Box

Buxus sempervirens 15m/50'
Habitat: Native. Grows on chalk and limestone in S. England. Also planted in gardens and churchyards, especially as a hedge.
Distribution: Native tree is rare in S. England; planted Box is common everywhere.
Similar species: Balearic Box *B. balearica* has dull leaves.

A tall tree with a long, straight trunk and angled branches which often curve upwards. In summer the crown looks sparser than on many trees. London Plane is easily recognised by its bark which peels off in large patches, and by its round, bristly fruits.

NOV-MAY

JUNE-NOV

Male and female flowers are on the same tree, in separate clusters

Shiny leaf

Large, broad leaf has pointed lobes

MAY

Greenish-yellow male flowers

Purplish female flowers in twos or threes

Round, bristly fruits, usually in pairs, stay on the tree all winter

SEPT-MARCH

Bark peels off in large patches giving the trunk a unique, patterned appearance

Smooth, slightly zig-zagged winter twig

Reddish buds have furry bases

London Plane

Platanus hybrida   35m/115'
Habitat: Introduced hybrid. Planted along roads and in parks, in towns and cities.
Distribution: Common in S. England and the Midlands; uncommon elsewhere.
Similar species: Oriental Plane *P. orientalis* (p47) and American Plane *P. occidentalis*: lobes of leaves are different. Maples (*Acer* spp. pp 72-75): fruit and bark differ.

46

NOV-MAY

This tree is usually shorter and broader than London Plane, with a thicker trunk. The crown is often rather irregular and the trunk may have knobbly swellings. The leaves are deeply divided with pointed lobes and the bark peels in rounded patches.

MAY-NOV

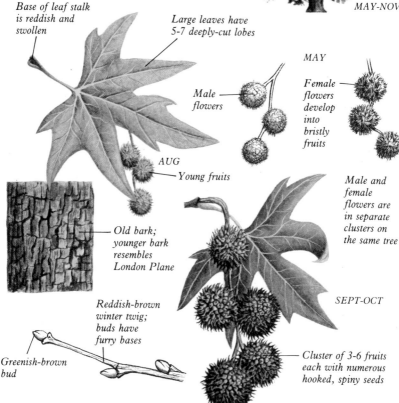

Base of leaf stalk is reddish and swollen

Large leaves have 5-7 deeply-cut lobes

MAY

Male flowers

Female flowers develop into bristly fruits

AUG
Young fruits

Male and female flowers are in separate clusters on the same tree

Old bark; younger bark resembles London Plane

SEPT-OCT

Reddish-brown winter twig; buds have furry bases

Greenish-brown bud

Cluster of 3-6 fruits each with numerous hooked, spiny seeds

Oriental Plane

Platanus orientalis   30m/100'
Habitat: Introduced from S.E. Europe. Usually planted in parks, not along roadsides. Does not survive well in cold areas.
Distribution: Uncommon in S. England; rare elsewhere.
Similar species: London Plane *P. hybrida* (p46): fruits and leaf lobes differ.

47

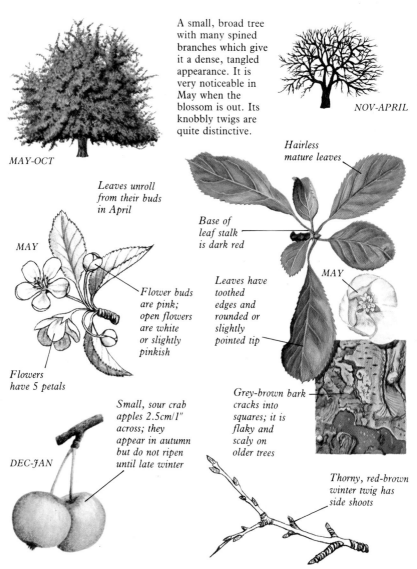

A small, broad tree with many spined branches which give it a dense, tangled appearance. It is very noticeable in May when the blossom is out. Its knobbly twigs are quite distinctive.

NOV-APRIL

MAY-OCT

Hairless mature leaves

Leaves unroll from their buds in April

Base of leaf stalk is dark red

MAY

MAY

Flower buds are pink; open flowers are white or slightly pinkish

Leaves have toothed edges and rounded or slightly pointed tip

Flowers have 5 petals

Small, sour crab apples 2.5cm/1" across; they appear in autumn but do not ripen until late winter

Grey-brown bark cracks into squares; it is flaky and scaly on older trees

DEC-JAN

Thorny, red-brown winter twig has side shoots

Crab Apple

Malus sylvestris   10m/33'
Habitat: Native. Found in copses, woodlands and hedgerows. Grows well on a variety of soils but likes a fairly light, open position.
Distribution: Frequent everywhere except in the northern half of Scotland.
Similar species: Apple *M. domestica* (p49) has larger, downy leaves and larger fruits.

48

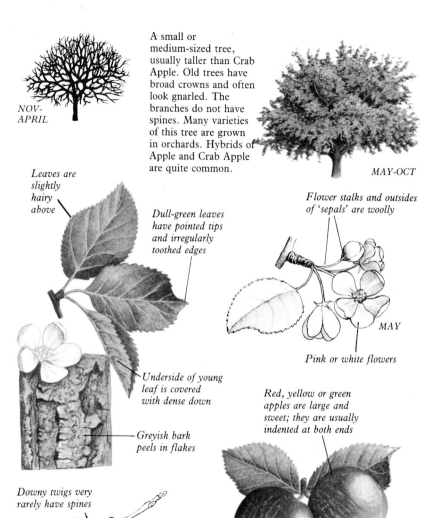

NOV-APRIL

A small or medium-sized tree, usually taller than Crab Apple. Old trees have broad crowns and often look gnarled. The branches do not have spines. Many varieties of this tree are grown in orchards. Hybrids of Apple and Crab Apple are quite common.

MAY-OCT

Leaves are slightly hairy above

Dull-green leaves have pointed tips and irregularly toothed edges

Flower stalks and outsides of 'sepals' are woolly

MAY

Pink or white flowers

Underside of young leaf is covered with dense down

Greyish bark peels in flakes

Red, yellow or green apples are large and sweet; they are usually indented at both ends

Downy twigs very rarely have spines

NOV-APRIL

SEPT-OCT

Apple

Malus domestica 15m/50'
Habitat: Cultivated tree. Grown in orchards and gardens for its fruit.
Distribution: Common as a planted tree throughout the British Isles and sometimes naturalized. Most commercial apple orchards are in S. and S.W. England.
Similar species: Crab Apple *M. sylvestris* (p48) has smaller leaves and sour fruit.

49

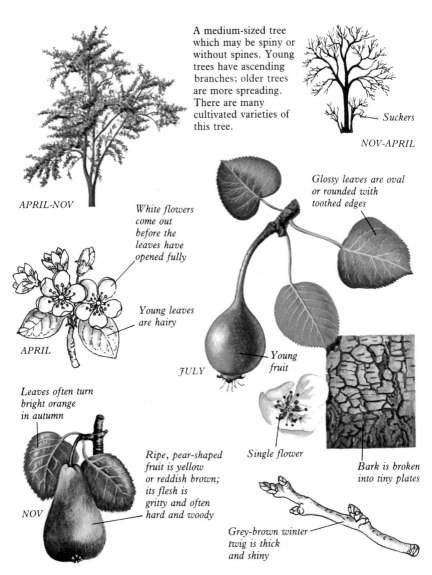

A medium-sized tree which may be spiny or without spines. Young trees have ascending branches; older trees are more spreading. There are many cultivated varieties of this tree.

Suckers

NOV-APRIL

APRIL-NOV

Glossy leaves are oval or rounded with toothed edges

White flowers come out before the leaves have opened fully

Young leaves are hairy

APRIL

JULY

Young fruit

Leaves often turn bright orange in autumn

NOV

Ripe, pear-shaped fruit is yellow or reddish brown; its flesh is gritty and often hard and woody

Single flower

Bark is broken into tiny plates

Grey-brown winter twig is thick and shiny

Common Pear

Pyrus communis   20m/66'
Habitat: Probably not native. Cultivated in gardens and orchards for its fruit. Also found growing wild in copses and hedgerows.
Distribution: Commonly planted throughout the British Isles.
Similar species: *Pyrus cordata* (found in S.W. England) has rounded fruits.

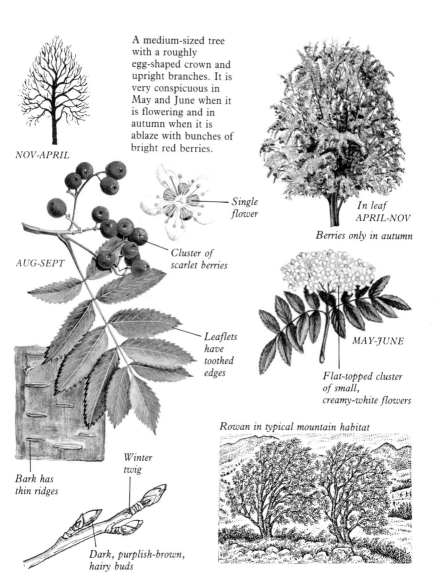

A medium-sized tree with a roughly egg-shaped crown and upright branches. It is very conspicuous in May and June when it is flowering and in autumn when it is ablaze with bunches of bright red berries.

NOV-APRIL

Single flower

In leaf APRIL-NOV

Berries only in autumn

AUG-SEPT

Cluster of scarlet berries

Leaflets have toothed edges

MAY-JUNE

Flat-topped cluster of small, creamy-white flowers

Bark has thin ridges

Winter twig

Dark, purplish-brown, hairy buds

Rowan in typical mountain habitat

Mountain Ash or Rowan

Sorbus aucuparia 20m/66'
Habitat: Native. Grows in woods, scrub and on mountains up to 1000m/3300'. Also planted in gardens and along roadsides.
Distribution: Common throughout the British Isles.
Similar species: Service Tree *S. domestica* (p55) has similar leaves but fruits differ.

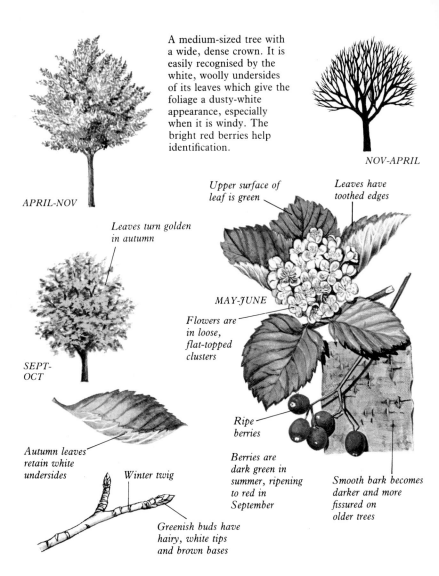

A medium-sized tree with a wide, dense crown. It is easily recognised by the white, woolly undersides of its leaves which give the foliage a dusty-white appearance, especially when it is windy. The bright red berries help identification.

NOV-APRIL

APRIL-NOV

Leaves turn golden in autumn

Upper surface of leaf is green

Leaves have toothed edges

MAY-JUNE

Flowers are in loose, flat-topped clusters

SEPT-OCT

Autumn leaves retain white undersides

Winter twig

Ripe berries

Berries are dark green in summer, ripening to red in September

Smooth bark becomes darker and more fissured on older trees

Greenish buds have hairy, white tips and brown bases

Whitebeam

Sorbus aria   25m/82'
Habitat: Native. Grows in woods or scrub on chalk or limestone. Planted in streets.
Distribution: Locally abundant as a native in S. England and central Ireland; rare as a wild tree elsewhere. Planted tree is common.
Similar species: Swedish Whitebeam *S. intermedia* (p53) has lobed leaves.

NOV-APRIL

A small or medium-sized tree with a broad, dense crown and a fairly short trunk. It is often planted in towns as it is very tolerant of air pollution. It has dark green, lobed leaves with grey, woolly undersides. In autumn, orange red fruits help identification.

APRIL-NOV

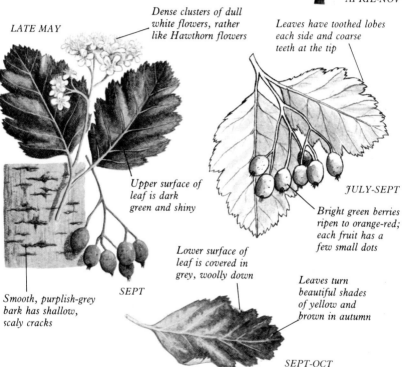

LATE MAY

Dense clusters of dull white flowers, rather like Hawthorn flowers

Leaves have toothed lobes each side and coarse teeth at the tip

Upper surface of leaf is dark green and shiny

JULY-SEPT

Bright green berries ripen to orange-red; each fruit has a few small dots

Lower surface of leaf is covered in grey, woolly down

Leaves turn beautiful shades of yellow and brown in autumn

SEPT

Smooth, purplish-grey bark has shallow, scaly cracks

SEPT-OCT

Swedish Whitebeam

Sorbus intermedia   15m/50'
Habitat: Introduced from Scandinavia. Planted in towns, on roadsides and in parks.
Distribution: Frequent throughout the British Isles.
Similar species: Whitebeam *S. aria* (p52). Service Tree of Fontainbleau *S. x latifolia* has similar foliage but larger leaves and yellow-brown fruits.

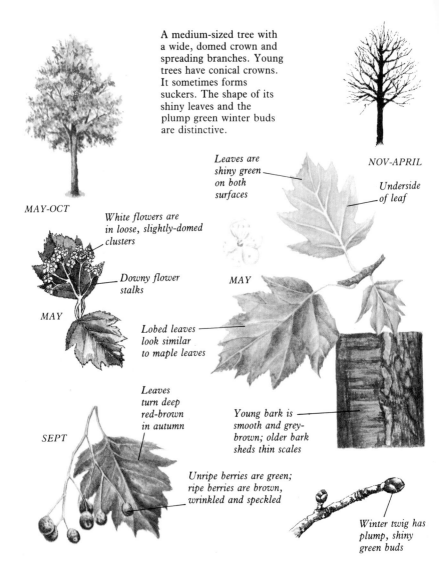

A medium-sized tree with a wide, domed crown and spreading branches. Young trees have conical crowns. It sometimes forms suckers. The shape of its shiny leaves and the plump green winter buds are distinctive.

MAY-OCT

NOV-APRIL

Leaves are shiny green on both surfaces

Underside of leaf

White flowers are in loose, slightly-domed clusters

Downy flower stalks

MAY

MAY

Lobed leaves look similar to maple leaves

Leaves turn deep red-brown in autumn

SEPT

Young bark is smooth and grey-brown; older bark sheds thin scales

Unripe berries are green; ripe berries are brown, wrinkled and speckled

Winter twig has plump, shiny green buds

Wild Service Tree

Sorbus torminalis   25m/82'

Habitat: Native. Grows in woods on clay or limestone soils.

Distribution: Uncommon in England and Wales, most trees occurring south of a line from the Humber to S. Cumbria; rare elsewhere.

Similar species: Maples (*Acer* spp): they have similar leaves but their fruits differ.

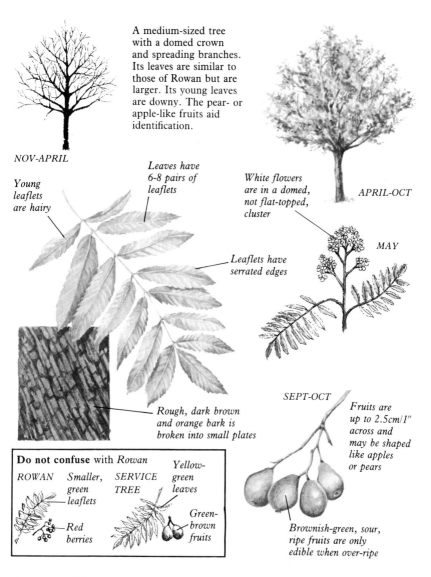

A medium-sized tree with a domed crown and spreading branches. Its leaves are similar to those of Rowan but are larger. Its young leaves are downy. The pear- or apple-like fruits aid identification.

NOV-APRIL

APRIL-OCT

Young leaflets are hairy

Leaves have 6-8 pairs of leaflets

White flowers are in a domed, not flat-topped, cluster

MAY

Leaflets have serrated edges

Rough, dark brown and orange bark is broken into small plates

SEPT-OCT

Fruits are up to 2.5cm/1" across and may be shaped like apples or pears

Do not confuse with *Rowan*

ROWAN — Smaller, green leaflets — Red berries

SERVICE TREE — Yellow-green leaves — Green-brown fruits

Brownish-green, sour, ripe fruits are only edible when over-ripe

Service Tree

Sorbus domestica   20m/66'
Habitat: Introduced from the Mediterranean. Planted in some parks and gardens.
Distribution: Rare. Most frequently seen in larger botanic gardens.
Similar species: Mountain Ash. *S. aucuparia* (p51) has similar leaves but smaller, red, berry-like fruits, and dark, purplish winter buds.

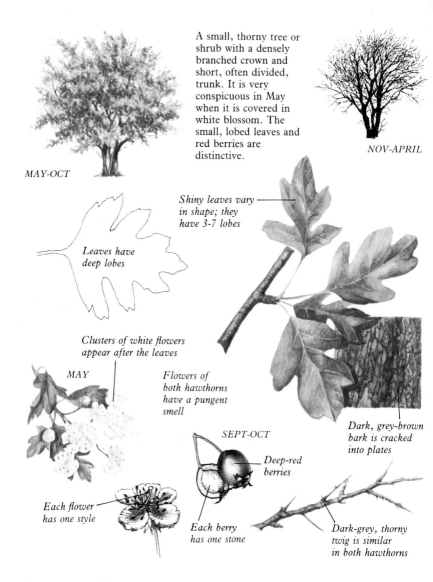

A small, thorny tree or shrub with a densely branched crown and short, often divided, trunk. It is very conspicuous in May when it is covered in white blossom. The small, lobed leaves and red berries are distinctive.

MAY-OCT

NOV-APRIL

Shiny leaves vary in shape; they have 3-7 lobes

Leaves have deep lobes

Clusters of white flowers appear after the leaves

MAY

Flowers of both hawthorns have a pungent smell

Dark, grey-brown bark is cracked into plates

SEPT-OCT

Deep-red berries

Each flower has one style

Each berry has one stone

Dark-grey, thorny twig is similar in both hawthorns

Common Hawthorn

Crataegus monogyna   10m/33'
Habitat: Native. Grows in hedgerows, woods and scrub on any type of soil. Also planted in gardens and occasionally in parks.
Distribution: Common throughout the British Isles except in extreme N. Scotland.
Similar species: Midland Hawthorn *C. laevigata* (p57): flowers and leaves differ.

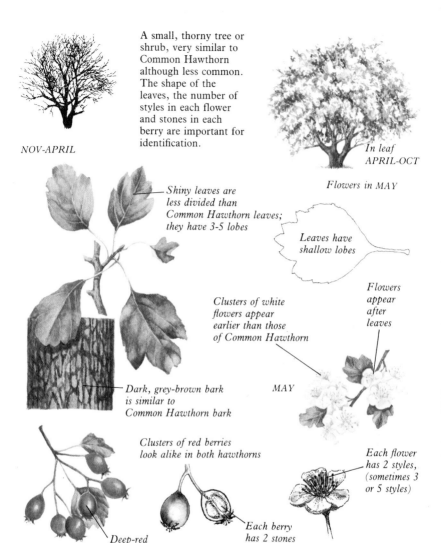

A small, thorny tree or shrub, very similar to Common Hawthorn although less common. The shape of the leaves, the number of styles in each flower and stones in each berry are important for identification.

NOV-APRIL

In leaf APRIL-OCT

Flowers in MAY

Shiny leaves are less divided than Common Hawthorn leaves; they have 3-5 lobes

Leaves have shallow lobes

Flowers appear after leaves

Clusters of white flowers appear earlier than those of Common Hawthorn

Dark, grey-brown bark is similar to Common Hawthorn bark

MAY

Clusters of red berries look alike in both hawthorns

Each flower has 2 styles, (sometimes 3 or 5 styles)

Deep-red berries

Each berry has 2 stones

SEPT-OCT

Midland Hawthorn

Crataegus laevigata   6m/20'
Habitat: Native. Grows in woods on clay soils. Less frequent in hedgerows.
Distribution: Locally abundant south-east of a line from the Humber to Swansea, occurring on suitable soils. Much less frequent than Common Hawthorn.
Similar species: Common Hawthorn *C. monogyna* (p56): flowers and leaves differ.

A dense, spiny shrub or small tree with a short, often forked, trunk and rounded crown. It usually grows upright. It is very noticeable in April when its dark branches are covered in pure white blossom, before the leaves emerge.

NOV-APRIL

MAY-OCT

Dark green leaves have toothed edges and are slightly hairy beneath

Delicate white flowers come out before the leaves

Oval, pointed leaf

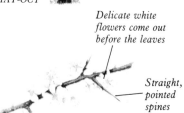

Straight, pointed spines

MARCH-APRIL

Ripe sloe

Reddish leaf stalk

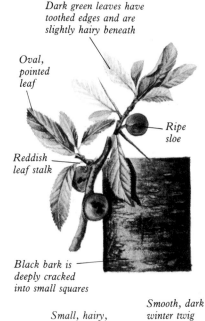

Fruits or sloes are green in summer; they turn purplish-black with a bluish bloom in September

Flesh of sloe has a very sour, astringent taste

Black bark is deeply cracked into small squares

Smooth, dark winter twig

Small, hairy, purple-black buds

SEPT-OCT

Blackthorn or Sloe

Prunus spinosa   6m/20'

Habitat: Native. Grows in hedges, woodlands and scrub on many kinds of soil.

Distribution: Common throughout the British Isles.

Similar species: Plum (p61) has larger, hanging, edible fruits and its flowers appear with the leaves. Cherry Plum *P. cerasifera* flowers in early March.

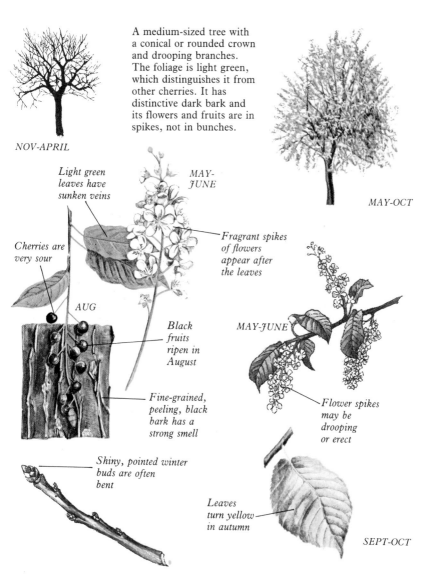

A medium-sized tree with a conical or rounded crown and drooping branches. The foliage is light green, which distinguishes it from other cherries. It has distinctive dark bark and its flowers and fruits are in spikes, not in bunches.

NOV-APRIL

MAY-JUNE

MAY-OCT

Light green leaves have sunken veins

Cherries are very sour

Fragrant spikes of flowers appear after the leaves

AUG

Black fruits ripen in August

MAY-JUNE

Fine-grained, peeling, black bark has a strong smell

Flower spikes may be drooping or erect

Shiny, pointed winter buds are often bent

Leaves turn yellow in autumn

SEPT-OCT

Bird Cherry

Prunus padus 15m/50'

Habitat: Native to British Isles except S. England. Planted in streets and gardens as an ornamental tree; grows in woods to an altitude of about 700m/2300'.

Distribution: Frequent in Scotland, Ireland, Wales and N. England.

Similar species: Black Cherry *P. serotina* has aromatic bark and dark, shiny leaves.

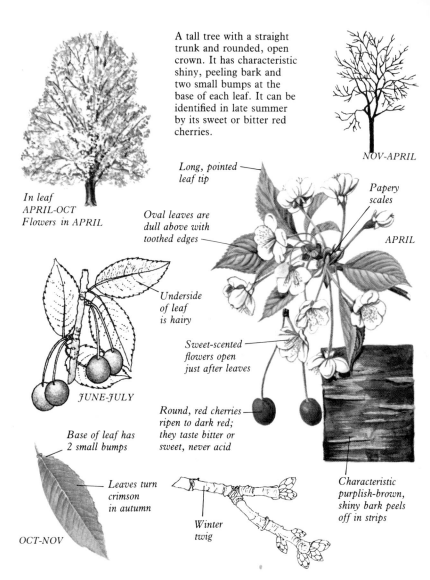

A tall tree with a straight trunk and rounded, open crown. It has characteristic shiny, peeling bark and two small bumps at the base of each leaf. It can be identified in late summer by its sweet or bitter red cherries.

NOV-APRIL

In leaf
APRIL-OCT
Flowers in APRIL

Long, pointed leaf tip

Papery scales

Oval leaves are dull above with toothed edges

APRIL

Underside of leaf is hairy

Sweet-scented flowers open just after leaves

JUNE-JULY

Round, red cherries ripen to dark red; they taste bitter or sweet, never acid

Base of leaf has 2 small bumps

Leaves turn crimson in autumn

Characteristic purplish-brown, shiny bark peels off in strips

Winter twig

OCT-NOV

Wild Cherry

Prunus avium   20m/66'
Habitat: Native. Grows in hedgerows and woods on all except the poorest soils. Often planted as an ornamental tree in gardens and parks.
Distribution: Common throughout the British Isles except in N. Scotland.
Similar species: Sour Cherry *P. cerasus* (p61).

60

NOV-APRIL

A bushy tree, similar to Wild Cherry but much smaller. When it is growing in the wild it often forms suckers. It has a rounded crown with drooping branches and scaly bark. It flowers in mid-May and produces acid-tasting cherries in summer.

APRIL-NOV

Finely-toothed leaf margin

Glossy, dark green leaves distinguish this from other cherries

Short, pointed leaf tip

MAY

Rounded petals

Clusters of white flowers appear later than Wild Cherry flowers

Leafy scales at base of flowers

JUNE-JULY

Cracked and broken greyish bark looks scaly on old trees

Ripe cherries are bright red; they taste acid, not sweet or bitter

Sour Cherry

Prunus cerasus   7m/23'
Habitat: Introduced from S.E. Europe. Grows in hedgerows and is planted as an ornamental tree in parks and gardens.
Distribution: Frequent in Wales, Ireland and S. England; rare elsewhere.
Similar species: Wild Cherry *P. avium* (p60).

61

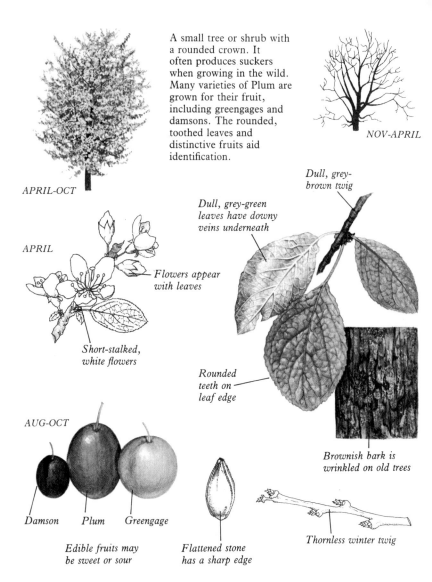

A small tree or shrub with a rounded crown. It often produces suckers when growing in the wild. Many varieties of Plum are grown for their fruit, including greengages and damsons. The rounded, toothed leaves and distinctive fruits aid identification.

APRIL-OCT

NOV-APRIL

APRIL

Dull, grey-brown twig

Dull, grey-green leaves have downy veins underneath

Flowers appear with leaves

Short-stalked, white flowers

Rounded teeth on leaf edge

Brownish bark is wrinkled on old trees

AUG-OCT

Damson   *Plum*   *Greengage*

Edible fruits may be sweet or sour

Flattened stone has a sharp edge

Thornless winter twig

Plum

Prunus domestica   10m/33'
Habitat: A cultivated tree of hybrid origin. It is grown in gardens and orchards and is occasionally naturalized in woods.
Distribution: Frequent throughout the British Isles.
Similar species: Blackthorn (p58). Cherry Plum *P. cerasifera* flowers in early March.

NOV-APRIL
Flowers in March

Young trees have upright branches and narrow crowns, older trees are wide-crowned and bushy. Almond is planted for its blossom as it rarely produces edible nuts in the British Isles. It is very susceptible to the disease 'Peach leaf curl'.

APRIL-OCT

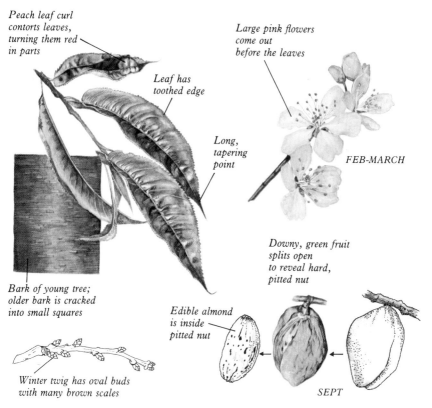

Peach leaf curl contorts leaves, turning them red in parts

Leaf has toothed edge

Long, tapering point

Large pink flowers come out before the leaves

FEB-MARCH

Bark of young tree; older bark is cracked into small squares

Winter twig has oval buds with many brown scales

Downy, green fruit splits open to reveal hard, pitted nut

Edible almond is inside pitted nut

SEPT

Almond

Prunus dulcis 9m/30'

Habitat: Introduced from N. Africa and S.W. Asia. Grown in S. Europe for its fruit but in the British Isles it is planted for its early show of flowers.
Distribution: Common in gardens throughout the British Isles.
Similar species: Peach *P. persica* has deep pink flowers and distinctive fruit.

An evergreen tree or shrub which is usually quite wide and bushy. It has a short trunk, which is often forked near the ground, and a dark green crown. Young branches are also dark green. The leaves do not smell aromatic when crushed. One of the most distinctive features of Portugal Laurel is the red colour of its twigs and leaf stalks.

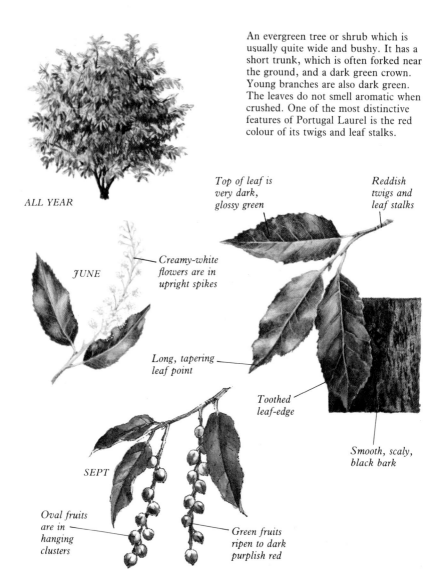

ALL YEAR

Top of leaf is very dark, glossy green

Reddish twigs and leaf stalks

JUNE

Creamy-white flowers are in upright spikes

Long, tapering leaf point

Toothed leaf-edge

Smooth, scaly, black bark

SEPT

Oval fruits are in hanging clusters

Green fruits ripen to dark purplish red

Portugal Laurel

Prunus lusitanica 12m/40'
Habitat: Introduced from Spain and Portugal. Planted in parks and gardens, often as a hedge or large shrub.
Distribution: Common throughout the British Isles, especially in S.W. England.
Similar species: Cherry Laurel (p65). Sweet Bay (p44) has aromatic leaves.

A wide, spreading evergreen tree or shrub with pale green young shoots. Like the Portugal Laurel, it is a popular garden tree, many varieties being grown. It has glossy green foliage and distinctively dark bark. The creamy-white flowers and berry-like fruits help identification. The crushed leaves smell strongly of almond.

ALL YEAR

Green leaf stalk

Large, glossy green, leathery leaves are lighter green than Portugal Laurel leaves

Creamy-white flowers are in shorter spikes than those of Portugal Laurel

APRIL-MAY

Short leaf point

Jet-black bark

Edges of leaves are often slightly inrolled

Round, berry-like fruits

SEPT

Fruits ripen from red to black

Cherry Laurel

Prunus laurocerasus   15m/50'

Habitat: Introduced from S.E. Europe. Often planted in parks and gardens and occasionally naturalized in woods.

Distribution: Common in gardens throughout the British Isles.

Similar species: Portugal Laurel (p64). Sweet Bay (p44) has aromatic leaves.

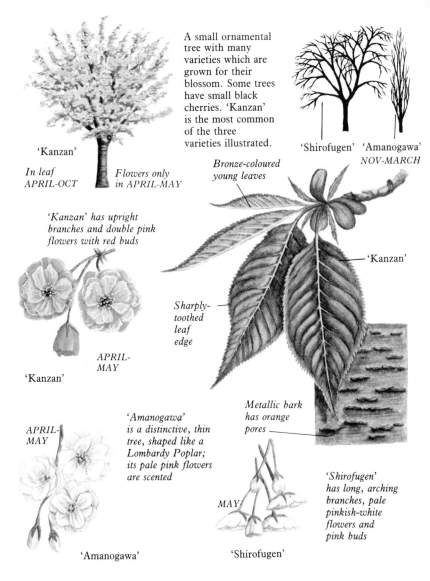

'Kanzan'

A small ornamental tree with many varieties which are grown for their blossom. Some trees have small black cherries. 'Kanzan' is the most common of the three varieties illustrated.

'Shirofugen' 'Amanogawa'
NOV-MARCH

In leaf
APRIL-OCT

Flowers only in APRIL-MAY

Bronze-coloured young leaves

'Kanzan' has upright branches and double pink flowers with red buds

'Kanzan'

Sharply-toothed leaf edge

APRIL-MAY

'Kanzan'

Metallic bark has orange pores

APRIL-MAY

'Amanogawa' is a distinctive, thin tree, shaped like a Lombardy Poplar; its pale pink flowers are scented

MAY

'Shirofugen' has long, arching branches, pale pinkish-white flowers and pink buds

'Amanogawa'

'Shirofugen'

Japanese Cherry

Prunus serrulata   9m/30'
Habitat: Introduced. Probably of Chinese origin but long cultivated in Japan. Grown here in parks and gardens as an ornamental tree.
Distribution: Common throughout the British Isles.
Similar species: Sargent's Cherry *P. sargentii* has small pink flowers.

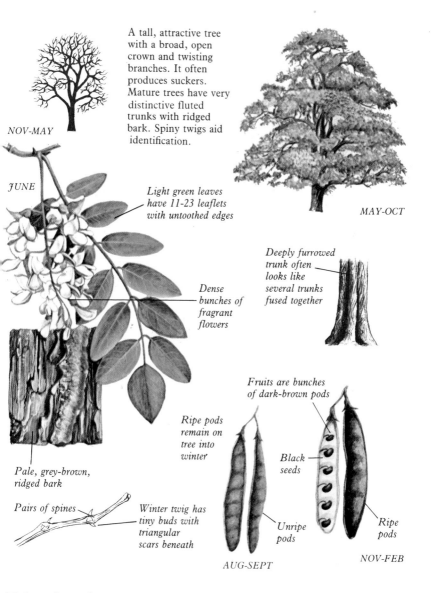

NOV–MAY

A tall, attractive tree with a broad, open crown and twisting branches. It often produces suckers. Mature trees have very distinctive fluted trunks with ridged bark. Spiny twigs aid identification.

JUNE

MAY–OCT

Light green leaves have 11-23 leaflets with untoothed edges

Dense bunches of fragrant flowers

Deeply furrowed trunk often looks like several trunks fused together

Pale, grey-brown, ridged bark

Fruits are bunches of dark-brown pods

Ripe pods remain on tree into winter

Black seeds

Pairs of spines

Winter twig has tiny buds with triangular scars beneath

Unripe pods

Ripe pods

AUG–SEPT

NOV–FEB

False Acacia

Robinia pseudoacacia   25m/82'
Habitat: Introduced from eastern North America. Grown in streets and parks.
Distribution: Common in S. England; uncommon in the rest of the British Isles.
Similar species: Honey Locust *Gleditsia triacanthos* has large, branched spines.

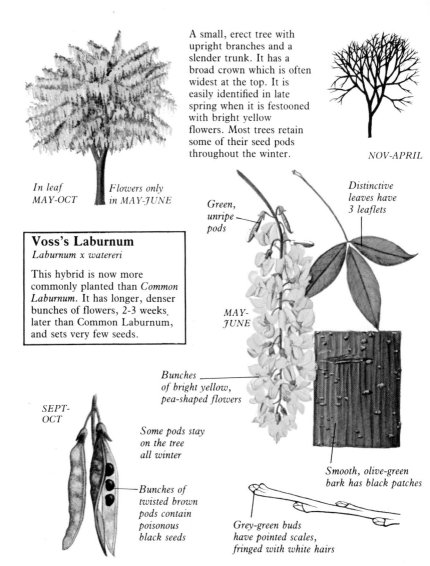

A small, erect tree with upright branches and a slender trunk. It has a broad crown which is often widest at the top. It is easily identified in late spring when it is festooned with bright yellow flowers. Most trees retain some of their seed pods throughout the winter.

NOV-APRIL

In leaf
MAY-OCT

Flowers only
in MAY-JUNE

Green, unripe pods

Distinctive leaves have 3 leaflets

Voss's Laburnum
Laburnum x watereri

This hybrid is now more commonly planted than *Common Laburnum*. It has longer, denser bunches of flowers, 2-3 weeks later than Common Laburnum, and sets very few seeds.

MAY-JUNE

Bunches of bright yellow, pea-shaped flowers

SEPT-OCT

Some pods stay on the tree all winter

Bunches of twisted brown pods contain poisonous black seeds

Smooth, olive-green bark has black patches

Grey-green buds have pointed scales, fringed with white hairs

Common Laburnum

Laburnum anagyroides   10m/33'
Habitat: Introduced from central and southern Europe. Planted here as an ornamental tree, especially in front gardens.
Distribution: Common throughout the British Isles.
Similar species: Scotch Laburnum *L. alpinum* has a longer inflorescence.

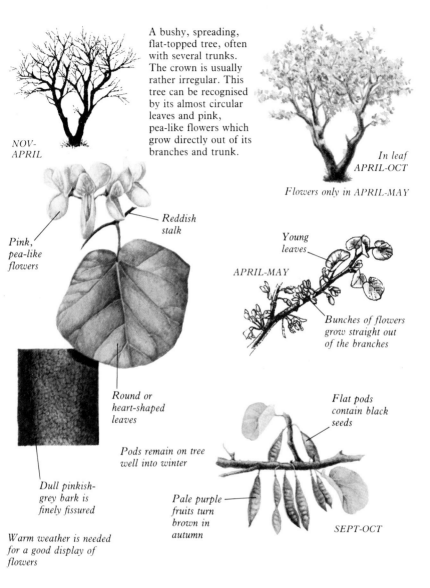

NOV-APRIL

A bushy, spreading, flat-topped tree, often with several trunks. The crown is usually rather irregular. This tree can be recognised by its almost circular leaves and pink, pea-like flowers which grow directly out of its branches and trunk.

In leaf
APRIL-OCT

Flowers only in APRIL-MAY

Reddish stalk

Pink, pea-like flowers

Young leaves

APRIL-MAY

Bunches of flowers grow straight out of the branches

Round or heart-shaped leaves

Flat pods contain black seeds

Pods remain on tree well into winter

Dull pinkish-grey bark is finely fissured

Pale purple fruits turn brown in autumn

SEPT-OCT

Warm weather is needed for a good display of flowers

Judas Tree

Cercis siliquastrum   10m/33'
Habitat: Introduced from S. Europe and the Middle East. Grown in parks and gardens.
Distribution: Uncommon in S. England; rare north of the Midlands.
Similar species: Katsura Tree *Cercidiphyllum japonicum* has leaves in opposite pairs.

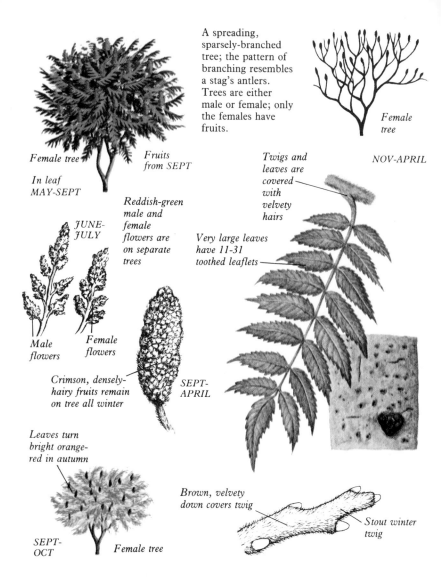

A spreading, sparsely-branched tree; the pattern of branching resembles a stag's antlers. Trees are either male or female; only the females have fruits.

Female tree

Female tree

Fruits from SEPT

In leaf MAY-SEPT

JUNE-JULY

Reddish-green male and female flowers are on separate trees

Twigs and leaves are covered with velvety hairs

NOV-APRIL

Very large leaves have 11-31 toothed leaflets

Male flowers

Female flowers

Crimson, densely-hairy fruits remain on tree all winter

SEPT-APRIL

Leaves turn bright orange-red in autumn

Brown, velvety down covers twig

Stout winter twig

SEPT-OCT

Female tree

Staghorn Sumac

Rhus typhina 8m/26′

Habitat: Introduced from eastern North America. Grown here mainly in gardens.
Distribution: Frequent throughout the British Isles.
Similar species: Varnish Tree *R. verniciflua* has untoothed leaflets.

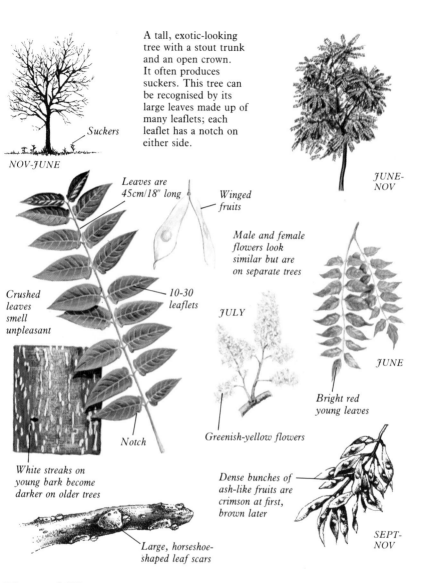

A tall, exotic-looking tree with a stout trunk and an open crown. It often produces suckers. This tree can be recognised by its large leaves made up of many leaflets; each leaflet has a notch on either side.

Suckers

NOV-JUNE

JUNE-NOV

Leaves are 45cm/18" long

Winged fruits

Male and female flowers look similar but are on separate trees

Crushed leaves smell unpleasant

10-30 leaflets

JULY

JUNE

Bright red young leaves

Notch

Greenish-yellow flowers

White streaks on young bark become darker on older trees

Dense bunches of ash-like fruits are crimson at first, brown later

SEPT-NOV

Large, horseshoe-shaped leaf scars

Tree of Heaven

Ailanthus altissima   25m/82'

Habitat: Introduced from China. Planted in parks, gardens and streets.

Distribution: Common in S. England, especially in London; rare in Ireland, Wales, N. England and Scotland.

Similar species: Downy Tree of Heaven *A. vilmoriniana* has downy, darker leaves.

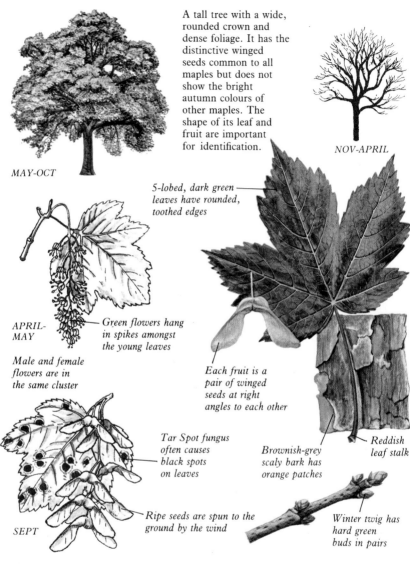

A tall tree with a wide, rounded crown and dense foliage. It has the distinctive winged seeds common to all maples but does not show the bright autumn colours of other maples. The shape of its leaf and fruit are important for identification.

MAY-OCT

NOV-APRIL

5-lobed, dark green leaves have rounded, toothed edges

APRIL-MAY

Green flowers hang in spikes amongst the young leaves

Male and female flowers are in the same cluster

Each fruit is a pair of winged seeds at right angles to each other

Tar Spot fungus often causes black spots on leaves

Brownish-grey scaly bark has orange patches

Reddish leaf stalk

SEPT

Ripe seeds are spun to the ground by the wind

Winter twig has hard green buds in pairs

Sycamore

Acer pseudoplatanus   35m/115'

Habitat: Introduced from Europe. Naturalized throughout the British Isles. Grows on roadsides and in woods on many soil types.

Distribution: Common throughout the British Isles.

Similar species: Other maples (*Acer* spp): leaf shape and angle of fruits differ.

NOV-MARCH

A tall, domed tree with a neat, rounded crown. It is very noticeable in spring when it is covered in bright yellow-green flowers, before it comes into leaf. The pointed lobes on its leaves distinguish it from Sycamore.

MAY-SEPT

Light green leaves have shallow lobes

Bunches of yellow-green flowers come out before the leaves

APRIL

Veins end in sharp points

Leaves turn yellow or orange in autumn

Fruits have a wide angle between their wings

OCT

Winter twig

Pale grey-brown bark has shallow ridges

Terminal bud is reddish brown

Green side buds

Fruits often persist on the tree into winter

Norway Maple

Acer platanoides   20m/66'
Habitat: Introduced from Europe. Planted in parks, gardens and in some streets.
Distribution: Common in S. England; frequent elsewhere. Less common than Sycamore.
Similar species: London Plane *Platanus hybrida* (p46): fruit and bark differ.

73

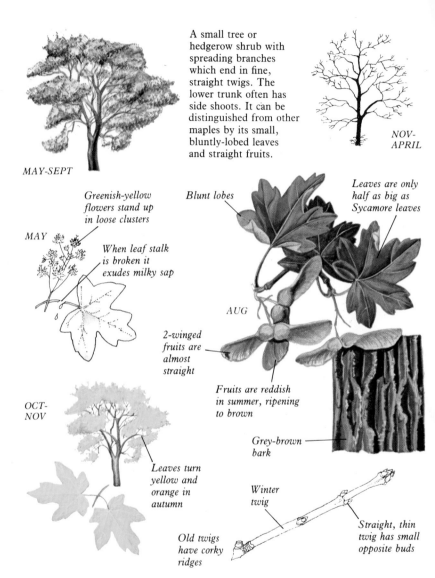

A small tree or hedgerow shrub with spreading branches which end in fine, straight twigs. The lower trunk often has side shoots. It can be distinguished from other maples by its small, bluntly-lobed leaves and straight fruits.

MAY-SEPT

NOV-APRIL

Greenish-yellow flowers stand up in loose clusters

Blunt lobes

Leaves are only half as big as Sycamore leaves

MAY

When leaf stalk is broken it exudes milky sap

AUG

2-winged fruits are almost straight

Fruits are reddish in summer, ripening to brown

OCT-NOV

Grey-brown bark

Leaves turn yellow and orange in autumn

Winter twig

Old twigs have corky ridges

Straight, thin twig has small opposite buds

Field Maple

Acer campestre   15m/50′

Habitat: Native to England and Wales. It grows in woods, hedgerows and in scrub, especially on calcareous soils. Planted elsewhere.

Distribution: Common throughout S. England and the eastern half of Wales.

Similar species: Sycamore *A. pseudoplatanus* (p72) has larger, pointed leaves.

74

NOV-APRIL

A small, bushy tree with a low, rounded crown and curved branches. There are many cultivated forms of this tree. Smooth Japanese Maple can be recognised by its small, deeply-lobed leaves.

MAY-SEPT

Leaves have 5-7 toothed lobes

Smooth bark

Dark, purple-red flowers are in upright clusters

In some varieties, flowers hang down

APRIL-MAY

Cultivars of Smooth Japanese Maple

Acer 'Atropurpurea' *has deep red-purple leaves*

Acer 'Dissectum' *has very deeply cut leaves*

Winged fruits are in erect bunches in most cultivars; they are green in summer ripening to pale red

JULY-OCT

Leaves turn bronze-red and purple in autumn

SEPT-OCT

Smooth Japanese Maple

Acer palmatum   6m/20'
Habitat: Introduced. Grown as an ornamental tree in parks and gardens.
Distribution: Frequent throughout the British Isles.
Similar species: Downy Japanese Maple *A. japonicum* has hairy, less divided leaves.

A magnificent tall tree with a thick trunk and a broad, spreading crown, especially when it is free-standing. It is very distinctive in May when it is covered in hundreds of white, candle-like flowers. The shape of its leaves is unmistakeable.

NOV-APRIL

In leaf MAY-OCT

Flowers in MAY

Leaves have 5-7 leaflets

Old leaf scars look like horseshoes

Candle of many flowers

Distinctive stout winter twig has a large, shiny terminal bud that becomes sticky in spring

MAY

Leaves turn yellow in autumn

SEPT

Husks split open to release shiny brown conkers

Young and old leaves hang down

Conkers may be round or flat-sided

Dark, grey-brown bark

Spiky green husk turns brown

OCT-NOV

Horse Chestnut

Aesculus hippocastanum   30m/100'
Habitat: Introduced from the Balkans. Planted in parks, gardens, streets and in town squares. Sometimes naturalized in woods.
Distribution: Common in England and Wales; frequent in Scotland and Ireland.
Similar species: Other *Aesculus* spp: buds, leaves and flowers differ.

76

This tree is a hybrid of Horse Chestnut and an American Buck-eye tree. It is smaller and less grand than Horse Chestnut, with smaller, crinkly leaves and red flowers. Its winter buds are not sticky and its fruits are spineless.

NOV-APRIL

Flowers in MAY

In leaf MAY-OCT

Leaflets may have short reddish stalks

Leaves are smaller, darker and more crinkled than Horse Chestnut leaves

Dark pink or red flowers

MAY

Leaves are shiny above

Fruits are smaller than Horse Chestnut fruits; they have few or no spines

OCT

Husks contain 2-3 nuts

Empty husk

Reddish-brown bark is often ridged and bumpy

Winter twig

Bud is not sticky

Small, dull brown nuts

OCT-NOV

Red Horse Chestnut

Aesculus carnea   25m/82'
Habitat: Hybrid of garden origin. Planted in streets, churchyards, parks and gardens. Grows best in an open, sunny position.
Distribution: Frequent in England and Wales; uncommon elsewhere.
Similar species: Other *Aesculus* spp: buds, leaves and flowers differ.

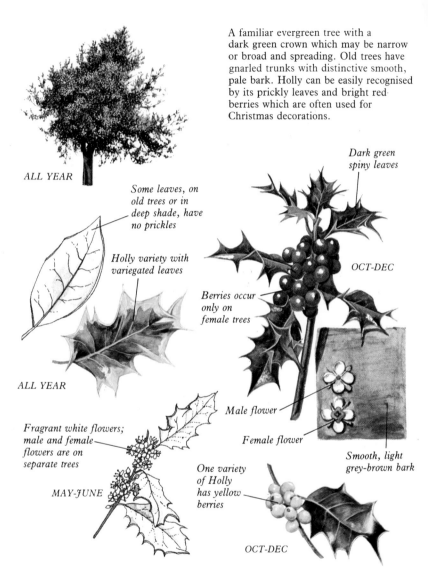

A familiar evergreen tree with a dark green crown which may be narrow or broad and spreading. Old trees have gnarled trunks with distinctive smooth, pale bark. Holly can be easily recognised by its prickly leaves and bright red berries which are often used for Christmas decorations.

ALL YEAR

Some leaves, on old trees or in deep shade, have no prickles

Holly variety with variegated leaves

ALL YEAR

Dark green spiny leaves

OCT-DEC

Berries occur only on female trees

Fragrant white flowers; male and female flowers are on separate trees

MAY-JUNE

Male flower

Female flower

One variety of Holly has yellow berries

Smooth, light grey-brown bark

OCT-DEC

Holly

Ilex aquifolium   20m/66'
Habitat: Native to most of the British Isles. Grows in hedgerows, woodlands and as scrub on hillsides. Grows on a variety of soil types.
Distribution: Common throughout the British Isles except in extreme N. Scotland.
Similar species: Some oaks (*Quercus* spp) have holly-like leaves.

78

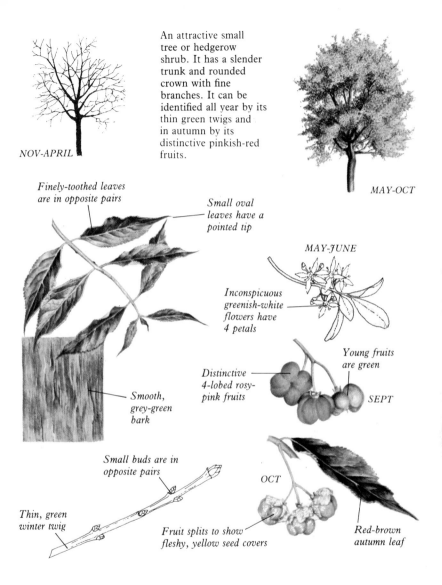

An attractive small tree or hedgerow shrub. It has a slender trunk and rounded crown with fine branches. It can be identified all year by its thin green twigs and in autumn by its distinctive pinkish-red fruits.

NOV-APRIL

MAY-OCT

Finely-toothed leaves are in opposite pairs

Small oval leaves have a pointed tip

MAY-JUNE

Inconspicuous greenish-white flowers have 4 petals

Distinctive 4-lobed rosy-pink fruits

Young fruits are green

SEPT

Smooth, grey-green bark

Small buds are in opposite pairs

OCT

Thin, green winter twig

Fruit splits to show fleshy, yellow seed covers

Red-brown autumn leaf

Spindle

Euonymus europaeus 5m/16′
Habitat: Native. Grows in woods, scrub and hedgerows, mainly on calcareous soils.
Distribution: Common in England, Wales, S. Scotland and Ireland.
Similar species: Broadleaved Spindle *E. latifolius* has larger leaves and berries.

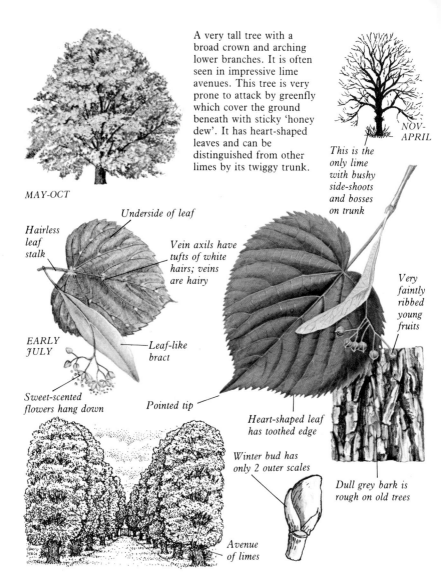

A very tall tree with a broad crown and arching lower branches. It is often seen in impressive lime avenues. This tree is very prone to attack by greenfly which cover the ground beneath with sticky 'honey dew'. It has heart-shaped leaves and can be distinguished from other limes by its twiggy trunk.

NOV-APRIL

This is the only lime with bushy side-shoots and bosses on trunk

MAY-OCT

Underside of leaf

Hairless leaf stalk

Vein axils have tufts of white hairs; veins are hairy

Very faintly ribbed young fruits

EARLY JULY

Leaf-like bract

Sweet-scented flowers hang down

Pointed tip

Heart-shaped leaf has toothed edge

Winter bud has only 2 outer scales

Dull grey bark is rough on old trees

Avenue of limes

Common Lime

Tilia x vulgaris   40m/130'
Habitat: Probably introduced from the Continent. Planted here in large parks, gardens and streets. Used for lime avenues on country estates.
Distribution: Common throughout the British Isles.
Similar species: Other limes (*Tilia* spp): fruits and undersides of leaves differ.

A large, handsome, towering tree with upswept branches. It does not have bosses or side shoots on its trunk. It can be distinguished from other limes by the bluish-green undersides of its leaves with rusty tufts of hairs.

NOV-APRIL

MAY-OCT

Long leaf stalk

Heart-shaped, toothed leaf

Hair-less leaf stalk

Fragrant flowers attract bees

EARLY JULY

Flowers are upright or spreading, not hanging

Underside is bluish-green with tufts of rusty-red hairs in vein axils

Leaf-like bract turns brown in autumn

Upper side of leaf is dark green and shiny

Red bud has 2 scales

Smooth grey bark

Small rounded fruits have no ribs

SEPT

Reddish, zig-zagged twig

Winter twig

Small-leaved Lime

Tilia cordata 30m/100'
Habitat: Native to England and Wales. Grows in woodlands, usually on limestone.
Distribution: Frequent throughout the British Isles.
Similar species: Other limes (*Tilia* spp): fruits and undersides of leaves differ.

An attractive large tree with spreading branches and no bosses or side shoots on its trunk. It has large, heart-shaped leaves which are hairy on both sides. Like other limes it has distinctive, leaf-like bracts on its flowers and fruits.

NOV-APRIL

MAY-OCT

Underside of leaf is hairy all over

Soft, hairy, heart-shaped leaves

Hairy leaf stalk

LATE JUNE

Unripe fruits

White tufts of hairs in vein axils

Hanging flowers appear earlier than those of other limes

Smooth, dark grey bark

Leaf-like bract

SEPT

Hairy, round to oval fruits have well-defined ribs; they are usually in threes or fours

Each dark red bud has 3 scales

Reddish twig is slightly zig-zagged

Large-leaved Lime

Tilia platyphyllos   30m/100'

Habitat: Possibly native in Yorkshire and the Wye Valley. Grows wild in woods on limestone. Planted in gardens and parks and as a street tree.

Distribution: Common throughout the British Isles.

Similar species: Other limes (*Tilia* spp): fruits and undersides of leaves differ.

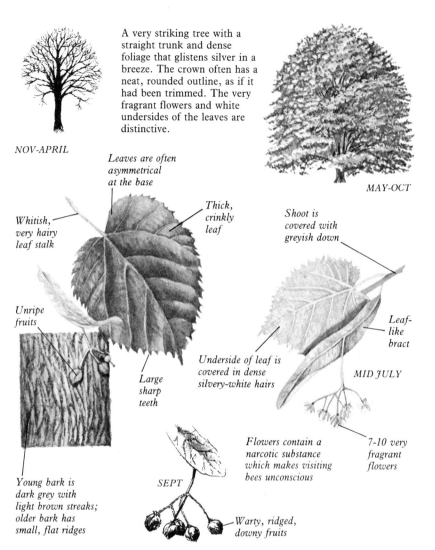

A very striking tree with a straight trunk and dense foliage that glistens silver in a breeze. The crown often has a neat, rounded outline, as if it had been trimmed. The very fragrant flowers and white undersides of the leaves are distinctive.

NOV-APRIL

MAY-OCT

Leaves are often asymmetrical at the base

Thick, crinkly leaf

Whitish, very hairy leaf stalk

Shoot is covered with greyish down

Unripe fruits

Leaf-like bract

Underside of leaf is covered in dense silvery-white hairs

MID JULY

Large sharp teeth

Young bark is dark grey with light brown streaks; older bark has small, flat ridges

SEPT

Flowers contain a narcotic substance which makes visiting bees unconscious

7-10 very fragrant flowers

Warty, ridged, downy fruits

Silver Lime

Tilia tomentosa   25m/82'
Habitat: Introduced from S.E. Europe. Planted in city parks and gardens.
Distribution: Frequent throughout the British Isles.
Similar species: Weeping Silver Lime *T. petiolaris* has pendent leaves on long stalks.

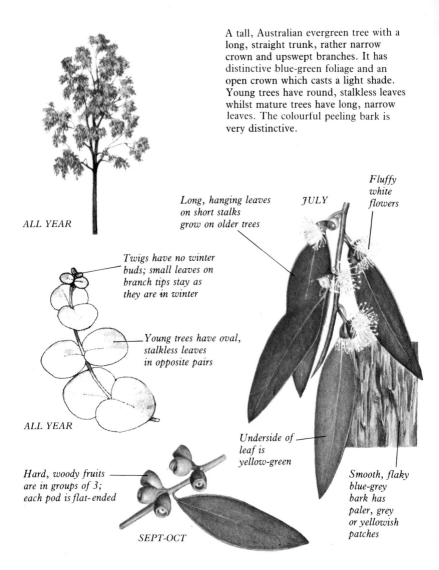

A tall, Australian evergreen tree with a long, straight trunk, rather narrow crown and upswept branches. It has distinctive blue-green foliage and an open crown which casts a light shade. Young trees have round, stalkless leaves whilst mature trees have long, narrow leaves. The colourful peeling bark is very distinctive.

Fluffy white flowers

Long, hanging leaves on short stalks grow on older trees

JULY

ALL YEAR

Twigs have no winter buds; small leaves on branch tips stay as they are in winter

Young trees have oval, stalkless leaves in opposite pairs

ALL YEAR

Underside of leaf is yellow-green

Hard, woody fruits are in groups of 3; each pod is flat-ended

Smooth, flaky blue-grey bark has paler, grey or yellowish patches

SEPT-OCT

Cider Gum

Eucalyptus gunnii 30m/100'

Habitat: Introduced from S. Australia. Planted here in botanical gardens.

Distribution: Uncommon. Most frequent in Ireland and near Britain's southern and western coasts. Rare elsewhere.

Similar species: Blue Gum *E. globulus* has long, dark, blue-green leaves.

A small evergreen tree with a dense, bushy crown and tough, leathery leaves. It has distinctive red shoots and rusty-red, flaking bark. This tree is most easily recognised in autumn when the round, strawberry-like fruits are ripe, and its bell-shaped, white flowers also appear.

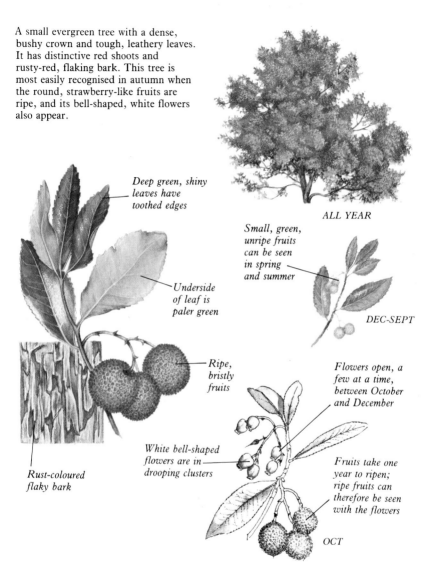

Deep green, shiny leaves have toothed edges

ALL YEAR

Small, green, unripe fruits can be seen in spring and summer

Underside of leaf is paler green

DEC-SEPT

Ripe, bristly fruits

Flowers open, a few at a time, between October and December

White bell-shaped flowers are in drooping clusters

Rust-coloured flaky bark

Fruits take one year to ripen; ripe fruits can therefore be seen with the flowers

OCT

Strawberry Tree

Arbutus unedo   10m/33′
Habitat: Native to S.W. Ireland. Also planted in gardens in sheltered places.
Distribution: Frequent in S.W. and W. Ireland; uncommon in the rest of Ireland, S.W. England and on the west coast of Scotland; rare elsewhere.
Similar species: Sweet Bay *Laurus nobilis* (p44) does not have reddish twigs.

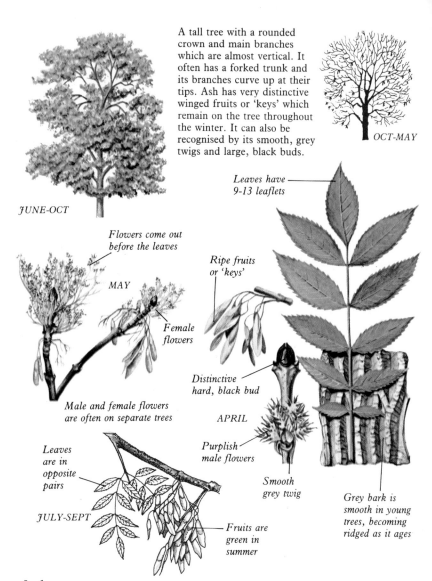

A tall tree with a rounded crown and main branches which are almost vertical. It often has a forked trunk and its branches curve up at their tips. Ash has very distinctive winged fruits or 'keys' which remain on the tree throughout the winter. It can also be recognised by its smooth, grey twigs and large, black buds.

OCT-MAY

JUNE-OCT

Leaves have 9-13 leaflets

Flowers come out before the leaves

Ripe fruits or 'keys'

MAY

Female flowers

Distinctive hard, black bud

Male and female flowers are often on separate trees

APRIL

Leaves are in opposite pairs

Purplish male flowers

JULY-SEPT

Smooth grey twig

Grey bark is smooth in young trees, becoming ridged as it ages

Fruits are green in summer

Ash

Fraxinus excelsior   40m/130'
Habitat: Native. Forms pure ash woodland on limestone in wetter regions and grows in mixed woods elsewhere. Often grows with oak in lowland areas.
Distribution: Common throughout the British Isles.
Similar species: Manna Ash *Fraxinus ornus* (p87): winter buds and flowers differ.

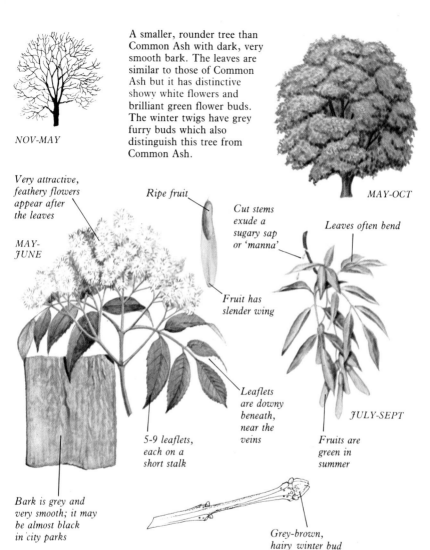

NOV-MAY

A smaller, rounder tree than Common Ash with dark, very smooth bark. The leaves are similar to those of Common Ash but it has distinctive showy white flowers and brilliant green flower buds. The winter twigs have grey furry buds which also distinguish this tree from Common Ash.

MAY-OCT

Very attractive, feathery flowers appear after the leaves

Ripe fruit

Cut stems exude a sugary sap or 'manna'

Leaves often bend

MAY-JUNE

Fruit has slender wing

Leaflets are downy beneath, near the veins

5-9 leaflets, each on a short stalk

JULY-SEPT

Fruits are green in summer

Bark is grey and very smooth; it may be almost black in city parks

Grey-brown, hairy winter bud

Manna or Flowering Ash

Fraxinus ornus   20m/66'
Habitat: Introduced from S. Europe. Planted here in parks and gardens.
Distribution: Frequent throughout the British Isles.
Similar species: Other ashes (*Fraxinus* spp): they lack showy white flowers.

87

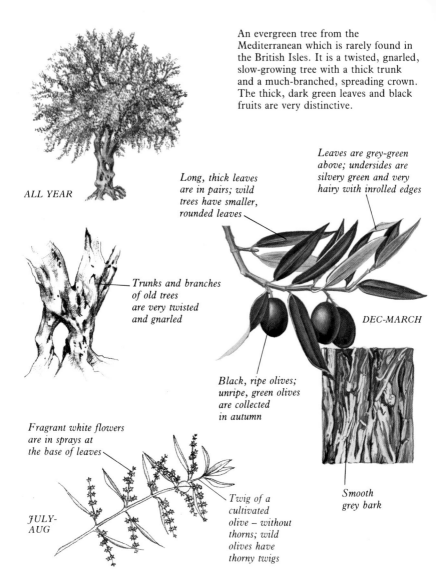

An evergreen tree from the Mediterranean which is rarely found in the British Isles. It is a twisted, gnarled, slow-growing tree with a thick trunk and a much-branched, spreading crown. The thick, dark green leaves and black fruits are very distinctive.

ALL YEAR

Long, thick leaves are in pairs; wild trees have smaller, rounded leaves

Leaves are grey-green above; undersides are silvery green and very hairy with inrolled edges

Trunks and branches of old trees are very twisted and gnarled

DEC-MARCH

Black, ripe olives; unripe, green olives are collected in autumn

Fragrant white flowers are in sprays at the base of leaves

JULY-AUG

Twig of a cultivated olive – without thorns; wild olives have thorny twigs

Smooth grey bark

Olive

Olea europaea 15m/50'
Habitat: Introduced from the Mediterranean region. Grown in sheltered gardens.
Distribution: Rare in the British Isles but found in a few gardens in S. England.
Similar species: Willows (*Salix* spp) have similar leaves but are deciduous.

NOV-APRIL

A small tree or tall shrub with a spreading crown, several trunks and characteristic forked branches. Lilac has very distinctive flowers, the remains of which can be seen on the twigs in winter. Winter twigs usually have two large terminal buds.

Several trunks   *MAY-OCT*

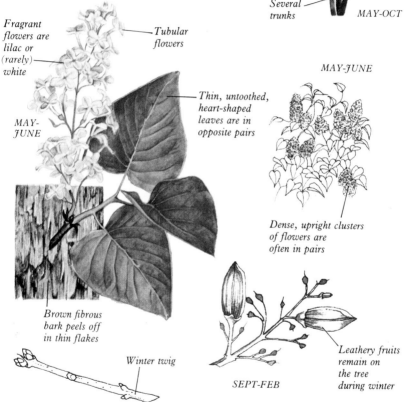

Fragrant flowers are lilac or (rarely) white

Tubular flowers

MAY-JUNE

MAY-JUNE

Thin, untoothed, heart-shaped leaves are in opposite pairs

Dense, upright clusters of flowers are often in pairs

Brown fibrous bark peels off in thin flakes

Winter twig

Leathery fruits remain on the tree during winter

SEPT-FEB

Lilac

Syringa vulgaris   5m/16′
Habitat: Introduced from S.E. Europe. Planted here as an ornamental in gardens.
Distribution: Common throughout the British Isles.
Similar species: Persian Lilac *S. x persica*: leaves and flowers differ.

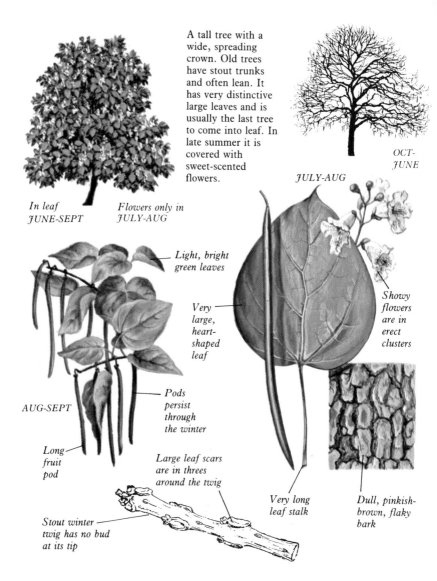

A tall tree with a wide, spreading crown. Old trees have stout trunks and often lean. It has very distinctive large leaves and is usually the last tree to come into leaf. In late summer it is covered with sweet-scented flowers.

OCT-JUNE

JULY-AUG

In leaf JUNE-SEPT

Flowers only in JULY-AUG

Light, bright green leaves

Very large, heart-shaped leaf

Showy flowers are in erect clusters

Pods persist through the winter

AUG-SEPT

Long fruit pod

Large leaf scars are in threes around the twig

Stout winter twig has no bud at its tip

Very long leaf stalk

Dull, pinkish-brown, flaky bark

Indian Bean Tree

Catalpa bignonioides   15m/50'
Habitat: Introduced from S.E. United States of America. Planted in parks and gardens.
Distribution: Frequent in S. England, especially London; uncommon elsewhere.
Similar species: Yellow Catalpa *C. ovata* has yellow flowers and leaves with three points. Western Catalpa *C. speciosa* has a narrow, not spreading, crown.

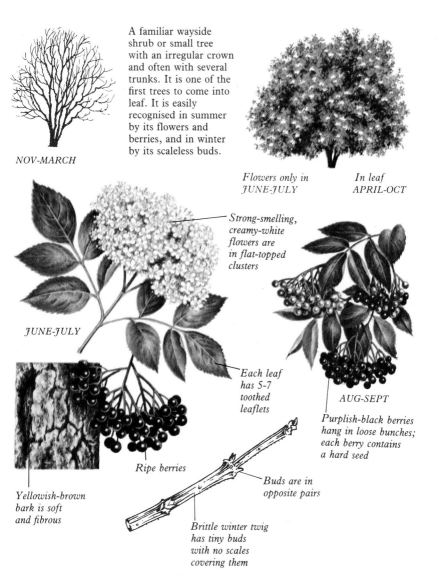

NOV-MARCH

A familiar wayside shrub or small tree with an irregular crown and often with several trunks. It is one of the first trees to come into leaf. It is easily recognised in summer by its flowers and berries, and in winter by its scaleless buds.

Flowers only in JUNE-JULY

In leaf APRIL-OCT

Strong-smelling, creamy-white flowers are in flat-topped clusters

JUNE-JULY

Each leaf has 5-7 toothed leaflets

AUG-SEPT

Purplish-black berries hang in loose bunches; each berry contains a hard seed

Ripe berries

Yellowish-brown bark is soft and fibrous

Buds are in opposite pairs

Brittle winter twig has tiny buds with no scales covering them

Elder

Sambucus nigra 20m/66'
Habitat: Native. Grows in hedgerows, scrub and open woods.
Distribution: Common throughout the British Isles except in N. Scotland.
Similar species: *Sambucus racemosa* has red fruit and ovoid flower clusters.

A small tree or shrub which often has more than one trunk. The woolly down on its twigs and leaves gives the tree a dusty appearance. The clusters of white flowers, oval berries and the distinctive winter twigs make it an easy tree to identify in any season.

NOV-APRIL

APRIL-OCT

MAY-JUNE

Thick, crinkled leaves

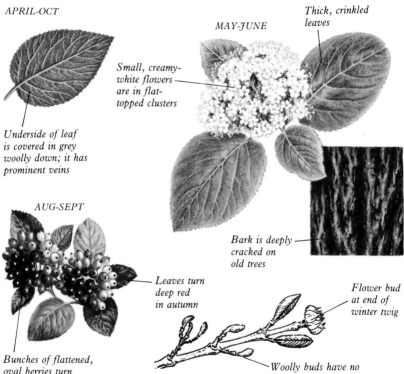

Small, creamy-white flowers are in flat-topped clusters

Underside of leaf is covered in grey woolly down; it has prominent veins

AUG-SEPT

Bark is deeply cracked on old trees

Leaves turn deep red in autumn

Flower bud at end of winter twig

Bunches of flattened, oval berries turn red then black

Woolly buds have no scales covering them

Wayfaring Tree

Viburnum lantana   6m/20'
Habitat: Native to England and Wales. Grows in hedgerows and on scrub on basic soils such as chalk and limestone.
Distribution: Common in S. England, less frequent further north; rare in Ireland.
Similar species: Guelder Rose *V. opulus* (p93): leaf shape differs.

NOV-APRIL

An attractive small, spreading tree or shrub with a dense, bushy crown and several trunks. It has maple-like leaves but can be distinguished from the maples by its distinctive clusters of flowers and red berries. The twigs have long, green terminal buds.

Flowers only in JUNE-JULY

In leaf APRIL-OCT

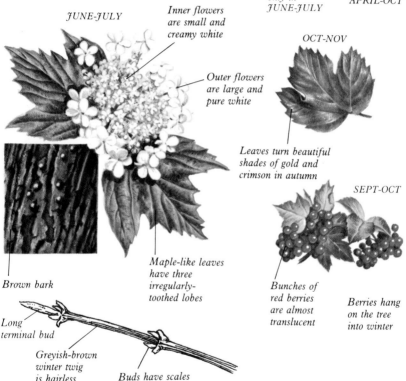

JUNE-JULY

Inner flowers are small and creamy white

Outer flowers are large and pure white

OCT-NOV

Leaves turn beautiful shades of gold and crimson in autumn

SEPT-OCT

Brown bark

Maple-like leaves have three irregularly-toothed lobes

Bunches of red berries are almost translucent

Berries hang on the tree into winter

Long terminal bud

Greyish-brown winter twig is hairless

Buds have scales

Guelder Rose

Viburnum opulus 4m/13'
Habitat: Native. Grows in hedgerows, scrub and in fairly open woodland. Thrives on damp soils in light situations.
Distribution: Common in England and Wales; uncommon in Ireland; rare in Scotland.
Similar species: Wayfaring Tree *V. lantana* (p92): leaf shape differs.

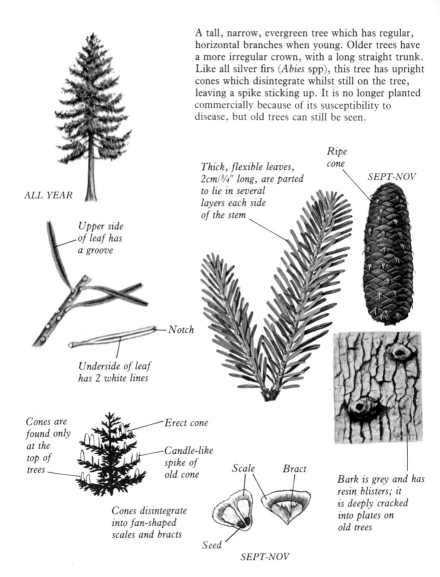

A tall, narrow, evergreen tree which has regular, horizontal branches when young. Older trees have a more irregular crown, with a long straight trunk. Like all silver firs (*Abies* spp), this tree has upright cones which disintegrate whilst still on the tree, leaving a spike sticking up. It is no longer planted commercially because of its susceptibility to disease, but old trees can still be seen.

ALL YEAR

Ripe cone

SEPT-NOV

Thick, flexible leaves, 2cm/³/₄" long, are parted to lie in several layers each side of the stem

Upper side of leaf has a groove

Notch

Underside of leaf has 2 white lines

Cones are found only at the top of trees

Erect cone

Candle-like spike of old cone

Scale

Bract

Cones disintegrate into fan-shaped scales and bracts

Seed

SEPT-NOV

Bark is grey and has resin blisters; it is deeply cracked into plates on old trees

European Silver Fir

Abies alba   50m/165'

Habitat: Introduced from the mountains of central Europe. Used in forestry plantations in the last century but now mostly an ornamental tree.

Distribution: Uncommon throughout the British Isles.

Similar species: Other silver firs (*Abies* spp): cone scales and foliage differ.

A tall, attractive conifer with decorative foliage and a silvery-grey trunk. Mature trees have a tapering trunk with a narrow, rounded crown. This is a silver fir with upright cones which disintegrate before falling; the woody scales which fall to the ground have distinctive bracts. The upswept needles are characteristic.

Tips of needles are rounded, not notched

ALL YEAR

Leaves are spiralled around the twigs, not parted

Silvery-green, leathery needles have whitish bands beneath

Leaves are upswept on side branches, especially near the top of the tree

Large cone, 20cm/8" long, has down-pointing bracts

MAY

SEPT-NOV

Pale, purplish-grey bark has resin blisters

Scale

Cones disintegrate into woody scales with long bracts

Bract

Small, bright red male flowers are crowded along the undersides of branches

SEPT-NOV

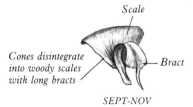

Noble Fir

Abies procera 80m/260'
Habitat: Introduced from western North America. Usually planted as an ornamental tree in parks and gardens; grown in plantations in W. Scotland.
Distribution: Frequent throughout the British Isles.
Similar species: Other silver firs (*Abies* spp): arrangement of needles differs.

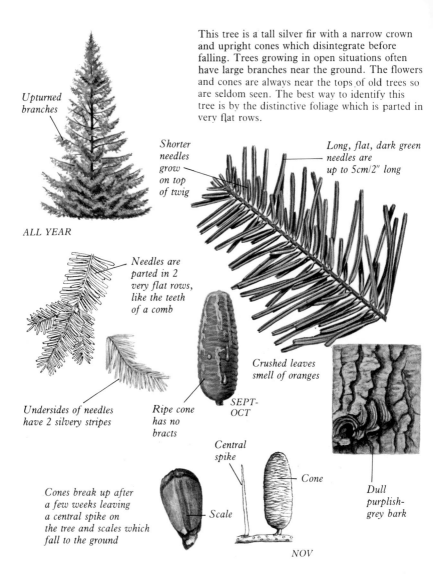

This tree is a tall silver fir with a narrow crown and upright cones which disintegrate before falling. Trees growing in open situations often have large branches near the ground. The flowers and cones are always near the tops of old trees so are seldom seen. The best way to identify this tree is by the distinctive foliage which is parted in very flat rows.

Upturned branches

Shorter needles grow on top of twig

Long, flat, dark green needles are up to 5cm/2" long

ALL YEAR

Needles are parted in 2 very flat rows, like the teeth of a comb

Crushed leaves smell of oranges

Undersides of needles have 2 silvery stripes

Ripe cone has no bracts

SEPT-OCT

Central spike

Cone

Dull purplish-grey bark

Cones break up after a few weeks leaving a central spike on the tree and scales which fall to the ground

Scale

NOV

Grand Fir

Abies grandis   75m/245'
Habitat: Introduced from western North America. Increasingly grown in plantations; also grown as an ornamental tree in large gardens.
Distribution: Frequent throughout the British Isles.
Similar species: Other *Abies* spp: they do not have needles parted in flat rows.

A tall, conical evergreen tree with a stout trunk and branches in regular whorls, usually right down to the ground. Caucasian Fir, like other silver firs, has upright cones which disintegrate into woody scales before falling. Its needles are not parted in rows but point forward on the twigs; the foliage smells fruity when crushed.

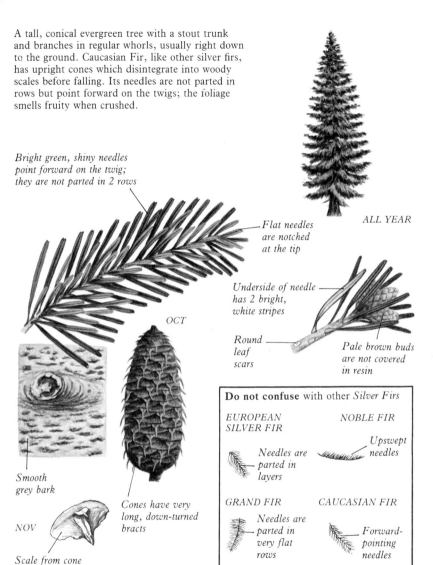

Bright green, shiny needles point forward on the twig; they are not parted in 2 rows

ALL YEAR

OCT

Flat needles are notched at the tip

Underside of needle has 2 bright, white stripes

Round leaf scars

Pale brown buds are not covered in resin

Smooth grey bark

NOV

Scale from cone

Cones have very long, down-turned bracts

Do not confuse with other *Silver Firs*

EUROPEAN SILVER FIR

Needles are parted in layers

NOBLE FIR

Upswept needles

GRAND FIR

Needles are parted in very flat rows

CAUCASIAN FIR

Forward-pointing needles

Caucasian Fir

Abies nordmanniana 70m/230'
Habitat: Introduced from the Caucasus region. Planted here as an ornamental tree in gardens. Not grown as a timber tree in plantations.
Distribution: Uncommon. Found in larger gardens throughout the British Isles.
Similar species: European Silver Fir *A. alba* (p94) has parted needles.

A tall, pyramidal conifer with heavy foliage and branches in irregular whorls. The lowest branches often bend almost to touch the ground, with their tips curving upwards. Douglas Fir looks like a silver fir but has very soft foliage and distinctive cones with 3-pronged bracts; the cones fall from the tree without breaking up.

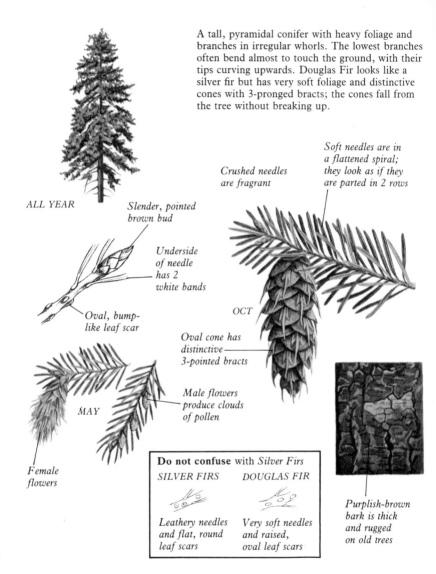

ALL YEAR

Slender, pointed brown bud

Underside of needle has 2 white bands

Oval, bump-like leaf scar

Crushed needles are fragrant

Soft needles are in a flattened spiral; they look as if they are parted in 2 rows

OCT

Oval cone has distinctive 3-pointed bracts

Male flowers produce clouds of pollen

MAY

Female flowers

Do not confuse with *Silver Firs*

SILVER FIRS   *DOUGLAS FIR*

Leathery needles and flat, round leaf scars

Very soft needles and raised, oval leaf scars

Purplish-brown bark is thick and rugged on old trees

Douglas Fir

Pseudotsuga menziesii   60m/195'
Habitat: Introduced from western North America. Grown here in forestry plantations and as an ornamental tree in larger gardens.
Distribution: Common throughout the British Isles, especially in the West.
Similar species: Silver firs (*Abies* spp): bracts on cones and leaf scars differ.

A tall, conical tree which looks rather graceful and elegant. The drooping leading shoot and branch tips make this an easy conifer to identify. The needles are of three different sizes and have rounded tips. In autumn, the tiny, oval cones can be seen at the tip of almost every twig.

Dark green needles are 3 different sizes

Long needle

Medium needle

Small cone is at tip of twig

ALL YEAR

Characteristic drooping top shoot

Branches are in irregular whorls

Short needle

SEPT-OCT

Underside of needle has 2 bluish-white bands

Rounded tip

Sparsely-set needles are parted in 2 rows

Needles grow from cushion-like bumps

Needles have a short stalk

Dark brown scaly bark

Reddish-purple female flowers

Yellowish-red male flowers

APRIL-MAY

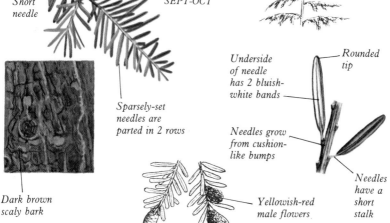

Western Hemlock

Tsuga heterophylla   50m/165'
Habitat: Introduced from North America. Grown in plantations and large gardens.
Distribution: Common in Scotland, Ireland and west of a line from Hexham to Weymouth; uncommon in eastern England.
Similar species: Eastern Hemlock *T. canadensis* has tapering needles.

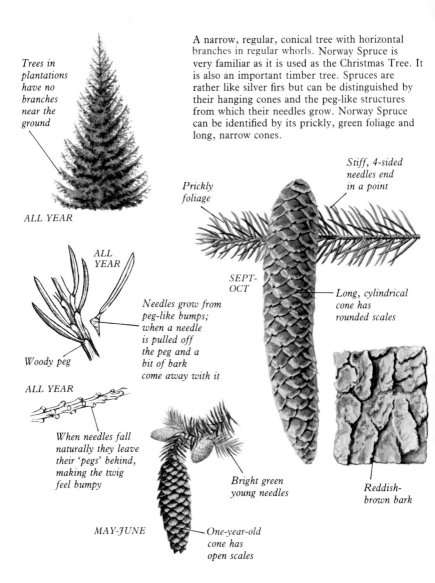

Trees in plantations have no branches near the ground

ALL YEAR

A narrow, regular, conical tree with horizontal branches in regular whorls. Norway Spruce is very familiar as it is used as the Christmas Tree. It is also an important timber tree. Spruces are rather like silver firs but can be distinguished by their hanging cones and the peg-like structures from which their needles grow. Norway Spruce can be identified by its prickly, green foliage and long, narrow cones.

Prickly foliage

Stiff, 4-sided needles end in a point

ALL YEAR

SEPT-OCT

Needles grow from peg-like bumps; when a needle is pulled off the peg and a bit of bark come away with it

Woody peg

ALL YEAR

Long, cylindrical cone has rounded scales

When needles fall naturally they leave their 'pegs' behind, making the twig feel bumpy

Bright green young needles

Reddish-brown bark

MAY-JUNE

One-year-old cone has open scales

Norway Spruce

Picea abies 40m/130'
Habitat: Introduced from N. Europe. Grown here in forestry plantations.
Distribution: Common, especially in plantations in lowland areas.
Similar species: Sitka Spruce *P. sitchensis* (p101) has blue-green needles.

A narrow-crowned, conical tree with a long, spire-like tip. Its branches are in regular whorls and usually droop on old trees. This tree has peg-like projections on its twigs making them feel bumpy. It can be distinguished from Norway Spruce by its distinctive, bluish-green foliage and by its smaller cones with crinkly scales. The foliage is very sharp and prickly.

Pale brown cone is half the size of Norway Spruce cone; scales have crinkly edges

SEPT-OCT

ALL YEAR

Stiff, flat needles have 2 silvery bands beneath

ALL YEAR

Needles end in a very sharp point making the foliage feel sharp and prickly

Needles are held on small 'pegs' (like Norway Spruce); pegs come away when the needle is pulled off

Bluish or grey-green foliage

Flaky, grey bark feels rough

Cones are on the ends of twigs, usually near the top of the tree

SEPT-OCT

Sitka Spruce

Picea sitchensis   50m/165'
Habitat: Introduced from western North America. Grown here in forestry plantations.
Distribution: Common in areas of high rainfall. It is the dominant tree in forests in N. and W. England, Wales, Scotland and Ireland.
Similar species: Norway Spruce *P. abies* (p100) has green needles and long cones.

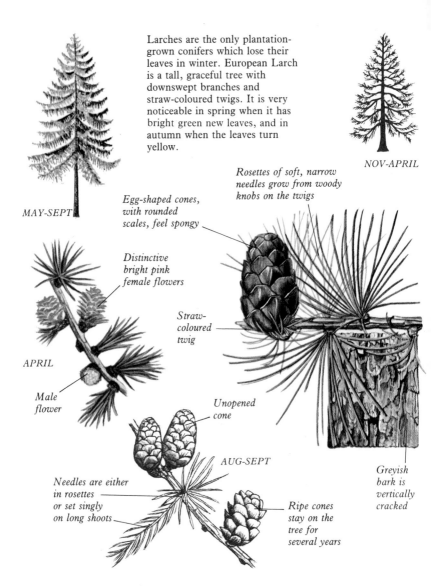

Larches are the only plantation-grown conifers which lose their leaves in winter. European Larch is a tall, graceful tree with downswept branches and straw-coloured twigs. It is very noticeable in spring when it has bright green new leaves, and in autumn when the leaves turn yellow.

NOV-APRIL

MAY-SEPT

Rosettes of soft, narrow needles grow from woody knobs on the twigs

Egg-shaped cones, with rounded scales, feel spongy

Distinctive bright pink female flowers

Straw-coloured twig

APRIL

Male flower

Unopened cone

AUG-SEPT

Greyish bark is vertically cracked

Needles are either in rosettes or set singly on long shoots

Ripe cones stay on the tree for several years

European Larch

Larix decidua   35m/115′
Habitat: Introduced from central Europe. Grown in plantations and as an ornamental.
Distribution: Common in England and Ireland; frequent in Wales and Scotland.
Similar species: Hybrid Larch *L. x eurolepis* (the hybrid of European and Japanese Larches) has characteristics intermediate between both parents and grows faster.

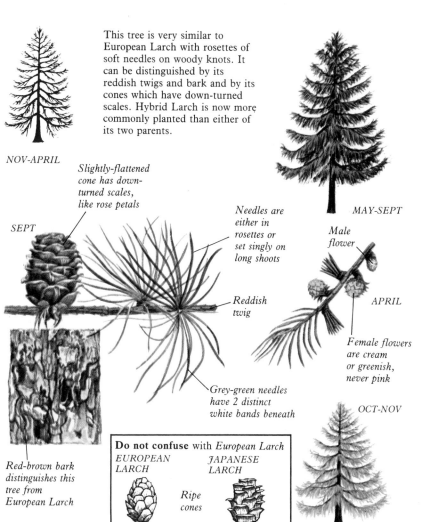

This tree is very similar to European Larch with rosettes of soft needles on woody knots. It can be distinguished by its reddish twigs and bark and by its cones which have down-turned scales. Hybrid Larch is now more commonly planted than either of its two parents.

NOV-APRIL

Slightly-flattened cone has down-turned scales, like rose petals

SEPT

Needles are either in rosettes or set singly on long shoots

MAY-SEPT

Male flower

APRIL

Reddish twig

Female flowers are cream or greenish, never pink

Red-brown bark distinguishes this tree from European Larch

Grey-green needles have 2 distinct white bands beneath

OCT-NOV

Do not confuse with *European Larch*

EUROPEAN LARCH

JAPANESE LARCH

Ripe cones

Scales may be wavy but not turned back

Scales are turned back like rose petals

Needles turn deep gold in autumn

Japanese Larch

Larix kaempferi   35m/115'

Habitat: Introduced from Japan. Grown in plantations in areas of high rainfall.
Distribution: Common in plantations in Scotland and Ireland and west of a line from Hexham to Weymouth. Frequent east of this line.
Similar species: Hybrid Larch *L. x eurolepis* grows faster than other larches.

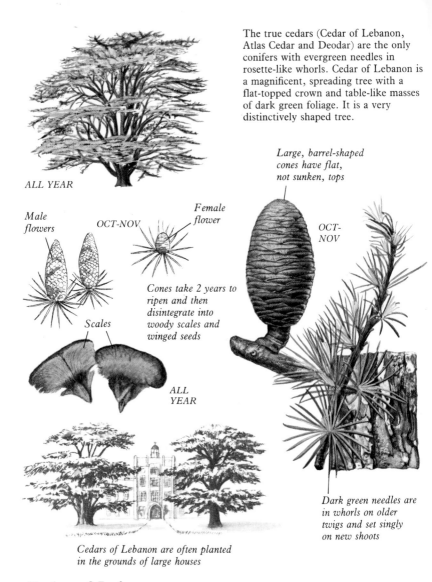

The true cedars (Cedar of Lebanon, Atlas Cedar and Deodar) are the only conifers with evergreen needles in rosette-like whorls. Cedar of Lebanon is a magnificent, spreading tree with a flat-topped crown and table-like masses of dark green foliage. It is a very distinctively shaped tree.

ALL YEAR

Large, barrel-shaped cones have flat, not sunken, tops

Male flowers

OCT-NOV

Female flower

OCT-NOV

Cones take 2 years to ripen and then disintegrate into woody scales and winged seeds

Scales

ALL YEAR

Dark green needles are in whorls on older twigs and set singly on new shoots

Cedars of Lebanon are often planted in the grounds of large houses

Cedar of Lebanon

Cedrus libani 40m/130'

Habitat: Introduced from Lebanon and S.E. Turkey. Planted as an ornamental tree in churchyards, cemeteries, parks and gardens, especially by large country houses.
Distribution: Common throughout the British Isles.
Similar species: Other cedars (*Cedrus* spp): crown shapes differ.

A broad, stately tree with widely-spaced branches which carry plates of foliage. It has a broad-based, conical crown and a sturdy trunk. Atlas Cedar is common in parks and gardens. An ornamental variety, with distinctive, blue-green needles, is often grown.

Cones take 2 years to ripen and then disintegrate on the tree leaving a central spike and woody scales

ALL YEAR

Shiny, blue-green needles end in a point

Unripe, green, barrel-shaped cones; cones usually have sunken tops

Upright cones

OCT-NOV

Leaves are in whorls on older twigs and set singly on new shoots

JUNE-AUG

Woody scales from cones

Winged seed

ALL YEAR

Do not confuse with other *cedars*
CEDAR OF LEBANON   ATLAS CEDAR

Tips of branches are level

Tips of branches ascend

DEODAR
Tips of branches droop

Atlas Cedar

Cedrus atlantica   40m/130'
Habitat: Introduced from the Atlas mountains of N. Africa. Planted here as an ornamental tree in large gardens and parks.
Distribution: Common throughout the British Isles.
Similar species: Other cedars (*Cedrus* spp): crown shapes differ.

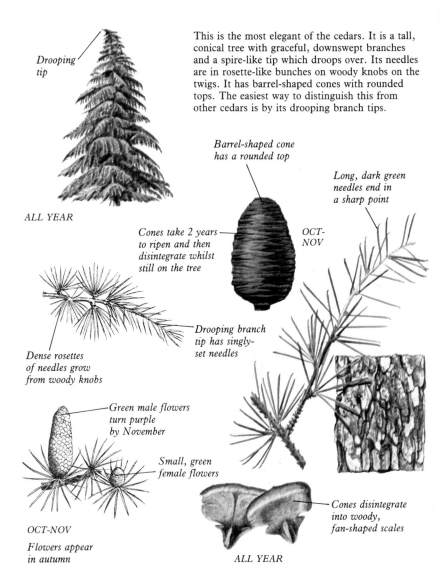

Drooping tip

This is the most elegant of the cedars. It is a tall, conical tree with graceful, downswept branches and a spire-like tip which droops over. Its needles are in rosette-like bunches on woody knobs on the twigs. It has barrel-shaped cones with rounded tops. The easiest way to distinguish this from other cedars is by its drooping branch tips.

ALL YEAR

Barrel-shaped cone has a rounded top

Long, dark green needles end in a sharp point

Cones take 2 years to ripen and then disintegrate whilst still on the tree

OCT-NOV

Drooping branch tip has singly-set needles

Dense rosettes of needles grow from woody knobs

Green male flowers turn purple by November

Small, green female flowers

OCT-NOV

Flowers appear in autumn

Cones disintegrate into woody, fan-shaped scales

ALL YEAR

Deodar

Cedrus deodara   60m/195'
Habitat: Introduced from the western Himalayas. Grown here as an ornamental tree in large gardens, parks and churchyards.
Distribution: Common throughout the British Isles.
Similar species: Other cedars (*Cedrus* spp): crown shapes differ.

A tall tree with a very straight trunk and a lightly-branched crown. Young trees are conical in shape; mature trees are narrow and flat-topped with distinctive, dark grey bark. It can be identified by its dark green, twisted, untidy-looking needles, held in pairs on the twigs. The cones take two years to ripen before falling whole from the tree.

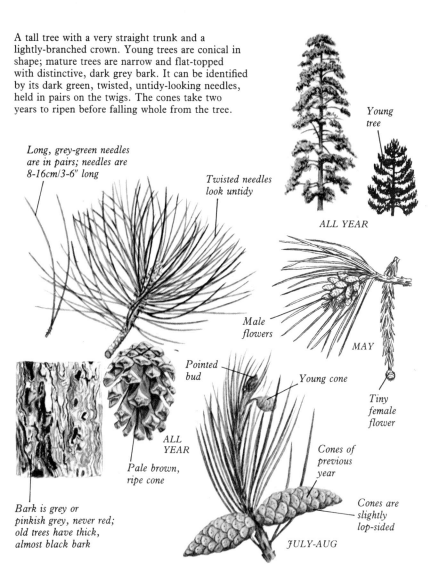

Young tree

Long, grey-green needles are in pairs; needles are 8-16cm/3-6" long

Twisted needles look untidy

ALL YEAR

Male flowers

MAY

Tiny female flower

Pointed bud

Young cone

ALL YEAR

Pale brown, ripe cone

Cones of previous year

Cones are slightly lop-sided

JULY-AUG

Bark is grey or pinkish grey, never red; old trees have thick, almost black bark

Corsican Pine

Pinus nigra subsp. laricio   40m/130'
Habitat: Introduced from Corsica and S. Italy. Planted for ornament and for timber.
Distribution: Common in plantations in S. and E. England, particularly in the New Forest and Thetford Forest; common in gardens and parks elsewhere.
Similar species: Austrian Pine *P. nigra* subsp. *nigra*: buds have loose, papery scales.

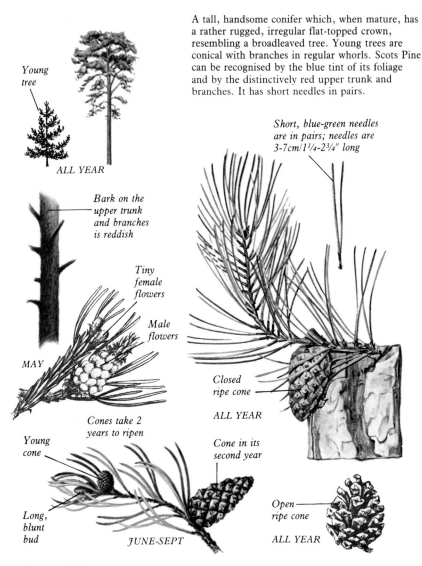

A tall, handsome conifer which, when mature, has a rather rugged, irregular flat-topped crown, resembling a broadleaved tree. Young trees are conical with branches in regular whorls. Scots Pine can be recognised by the blue tint of its foliage and by the distinctively red upper trunk and branches. It has short needles in pairs.

Young tree

ALL YEAR

Short, blue-green needles are in pairs; needles are 3-7cm/1¼-2¾" long

Bark on the upper trunk and branches is reddish

Tiny female flowers

Male flowers

MAY

Closed ripe cone

ALL YEAR

Cones take 2 years to ripen

Young cone

Cone in its second year

Long, blunt bud

JUNE-SEPT

Open ripe cone

ALL YEAR

Scots Pine

Pinus sylvestris   40m/130'
Habitat: Native to Scotland. Grows in open woods in Scotland and forms woods on sandy soils in S. England. Also grown for ornament and in forestry plantations.
Distribution: Common throughout the British Isles, especially in the Midlands and E. England as a forest tree, notably in Thetford Forest and Cannock Chase.

An attractive conifer with the longest needles of any 2-needled pine. Mature trees have long, bare trunks and horizontal branches which are widely spaced, giving the crown an open appearance. It has distinctive, large, shiny cones which are often clustered at the tips of the branches.

Young tree

Very large cones (up to 18cm/7" long) are light brown and shiny

ALL YEAR

Long, very stiff, grey-green needles are in pairs; needles are 10-25cm/4-10" long

ALL YEAR

Needles and cones are often clustered at the ends of twigs

Female flower

Red-brown bud

Male flowers

Reddish-brown bark is deeply cracked

Ripe, open cone; cones take 2 years to ripen

MAY

ALL YEAR

Maritime Pine

Pinus pinaster   40m/130'

Habitat: Introduced from the Mediterranean coastal region. Often planted as a windbreak, especially on sandy soils. Also planted to stabilize sand dunes.

Distribution: Common in S. England; rare in the rest of Britain and in Ireland.

A tall, rather narrow conifer with a dense, bushy crown and a long, straight trunk. Young trees are conical, often with bushy bases and spire-like tops. The very distinctive cones with sharp prickles distinguish Lodgepole Pine from the other pines. The short, mid-green needles are held in pairs.

Young tree

ALL YEAR

Bud

JUNE-APRIL

Ripe cones are shiny, pale brown

Sharp prickles

Needles are short; 3-7cm/1¼-2¾" long

Cones in their first year are very small

ALL YEAR

Long, blunt bud

Mid-green needles are in pairs

Cones take 2 years to ripen; unripe cones are green and prickly

Cones are often in pairs

Dark, grey-brown bark is flaky and quite smooth

Lodgepole or Shore Pine

Pinus contorta   25m/82'
Habitat: Introduced from western North America. Grown in forestry plantations in N. Wales and on peat bogs in Scotland. Not planted as an ornamental tree.
Distribution: Common in N. Scotland, N. Wales and Ireland; uncommon in southern and eastern Britain. Now the major species in plantations on peat bogs.

A tall tree with a high, domed crown and many branches which reach far down the trunk. Young trees are conical. The needles are held in bunches of three. The cones are in groups of three to five and are often held on the tree for as long as thirty years.

Young tree

Long, slender, soft needles are 10-15cm/ 4-6" long

Needles are in groups of 3

ALL YEAR

Female flowers are in clusters of 3-5

Young needles are grass-green

Large sticky buds are abruptly pointed

APRIL

Pale brown cone is very lop-sided at its base

MARCH-APRIL

Male flowers appear earlier than those of other pines

Thick, deeply-fissured grey bark

Cones may stay closed for many years

ALL YEAR

Ripe cones do not open fully

Monterey Pine

Pinus radiata 40m/130'
Habitat: Introduced from the Monterey area of California. Planted as an ornamental tree and increasingly planted for timber. Does not tolerate frost.
Distribution: Frequent in S.W. England, Ireland and W. Scotland; rare elsewhere.

A tall, narrow, rather tower-like tree with short horizontal branches which turn up at their tips. Branches are usually retained near the base of the trunk, even on old trees. Arolla Pine can be identified by its short, dark green needles which are held in bunches of five, and by its unusual cones which are plum-coloured when young.

Short needles are in bunches of 5; needles are 5-8cm/2-3" long

Dark green needles have bluish-white inner surface

ALL YEAR

Dense, forward-pointing needles

Male flowers

Female flower is on tip of new shoot

MAY

ALL YEAR

Young cones are purplish or plum-coloured

Shiny, red-brown, ripe cone does not open but rots to release seeds

Reddish-grey, scaly bark

Large, edible seeds

JULY-SEPT

Arolla or Swiss Stone Pine

Pinus cembra   25m/82'
Habitat: Introduced from the Alps. Planted here as an ornamental tree in larger parks and gardens. Not grown in forestry plantations.
Distribution: Frequent throughout the British Isles.

A fine-looking tree with very slender needles in bunches of five. It has a narrow crown with level branches which turn up at their tips. Young trees are conical and rather open; very old trees are often flat-topped. It can be distinguished from other pines by its very fine foliage and long, thin, slightly curved cones.

Young tree

Thin, blue-green needles are in bunches of 5; needles are 5-14cm/2-5½" long

ALL YEAR

Small clusters of male flowers are yellow when ripe

MAY

Slender, pinkish female flowers

ALL YEAR

Cylindrical ripe cone has widely-spaced scales; cones are often curved near their tip

JULY-SEPT

Bark from a young tree

Thick, fissured bark from an older tree

Twigs are usually hairless

Young, green cones; all cones hang down

White or Weymouth Pine

Pinus strobus 50m/165'
Habitat: Introduced from eastern North America. Once planted for timber but suffered from disease. Planted in parks and larger gardens as an ornamental tree.
Distribution: Frequent throughout the British Isles; more common in the South.

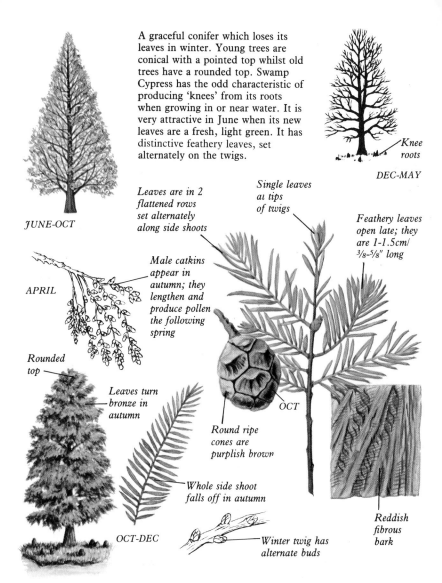

A graceful conifer which loses its leaves in winter. Young trees are conical with a pointed top whilst old trees have a rounded top. Swamp Cypress has the odd characteristic of producing 'knees' from its roots when growing in or near water. It is very attractive in June when its new leaves are a fresh, light green. It has distinctive feathery leaves, set alternately on the twigs.

Knee roots

DEC-MAY

JUNE-OCT

Leaves are in 2 flattened rows set alternately along side shoots

Single leaves at tips of twigs

Feathery leaves open late; they are 1-1.5cm/ 3/8-5/8" long

Male catkins appear in autumn; they lengthen and produce pollen the following spring

APRIL

Rounded top

Leaves turn bronze in autumn

OCT

Round ripe cones are purplish brown

Whole side shoot falls off in autumn

Reddish fibrous bark

OCT-DEC

Winter twig has alternate buds

Swamp Cypress

Taxodium distichum   30m/100′
Habitat: Introduced from S.E. United States of America. Planted here as an ornamental tree in parks and large gardens. Grows well on wet or dry soils.
Distribution: Frequent in S. England; rare in the rest of the British Isles.
Similar species: Dawn Redwood *Metasequoia glyptostroboides* (p115): leaves differ.

This conifer was introduced from China in the late 1940s, so only young trees can be seen in Britain. It is a fairly tall, conical tree which loses its leaves in winter, and has bright green new leaves in early May. It is very similar to Swamp Cypress but has longer leaves, in opposite pairs. It has distinctive winter twigs with leaf scars above its buds.

MAY-OCT

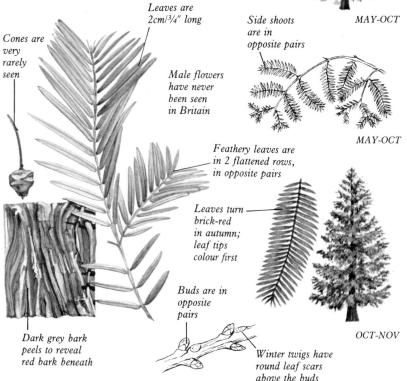

Leaves are 2cm/¾" long

Side shoots are in opposite pairs

Cones are very rarely seen

Male flowers have never been seen in Britain

MAY-OCT

Feathery leaves are in 2 flattened rows, in opposite pairs

Leaves turn brick-red in autumn; leaf tips colour first

Buds are in opposite pairs

OCT-NOV

Dark grey bark peels to reveal red bark beneath

Winter twigs have round leaf scars above the buds

Dawn Redwood

Metasequoia glyptostroboides   20m/66'
Habitat: Introduced from Szechwan in China. Planted here in many large gardens and parks where it grows best on damp soils.
Distribution: Frequent in gardens and parks in S. England; uncommon elsewhere.
Similar species: Swamp Cypress *Taxodium distichum* (p114): leaves differ.

In its native California this is the world's tallest tree. In Britain it does not reach such great heights but is still a tall, impressive tree. It has a straight trunk with a narrow, column-like crown and spreading or drooping branches. The most distinctive feature of this tree is its spongy, red-brown bark. It has two kinds of leaves; small, scale-like leaves and flat needles.

ALL YEAR

Leaves on small twigs are flat needles parted in 2 rows

Scale-like leaves are in spirals around the main shoots

Cones ripen in their first year

MARCH-APRIL

Scales of winter buds persist on twigs

Male flower

Small, egg-shaped cone is 2cm/3/4" long

Straight trunk spreads out at its base

Characteristic fibrous, spongy, red-brown bark

APRIL

SEPT-OCT

Female flower

Base of trunk often has twiggy shoots

Coast Redwood

Sequoia sempervirens   35m/115'

Habitat: Introduced from the coastal region of California. Planted in parks as an ornamental tree. Sometimes planted around forestry plantations.

Distribution: Common throughout the British Isles; less frequent in the North.

Similar species: Wellingtonia *Sequoiadendron giganteum* (p117): foliage differs.

116

A majestic tree which often towers above other trees in a park. It has a symmetrical, conical crown with down-swept branches and dark green foliage. It is similar to Coast Redwood, with spongy, fibrous bark on its massive trunk, but can be distinguished by its foliage which consists only of scale-like leaves. The cones are much larger than those of Coast Redwood.

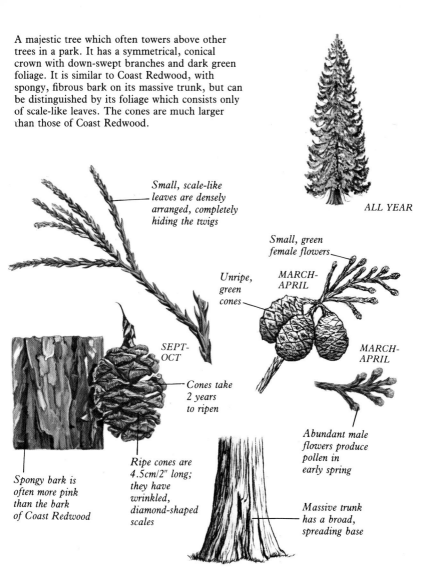

ALL YEAR

Small, scale-like leaves are densely arranged, completely hiding the twigs

Small, green female flowers

Unripe, green cones

MARCH-APRIL

SEPT-OCT

Cones take 2 years to ripen

MARCH-APRIL

Abundant male flowers produce pollen in early spring

Spongy bark is often more pink than the bark of Coast Redwood

Ripe cones are 4.5cm/2" long; they have wrinkled, diamond-shaped scales

Massive trunk has a broad, spreading base

Wellingtonia or Giant Redwood

Sequoiadendron giganteum   40m/130'
Habitat: Introduced from the Sierra Nevada, California. Planted in parks and gardens for ornament. Used as an avenue tree on country estates.
Distribution: Common throughout the British Isles except N. Scotland and W. Ireland.
Similar species: Coast Redwood *Sequoia sempervirens* (p116): leaves differ.

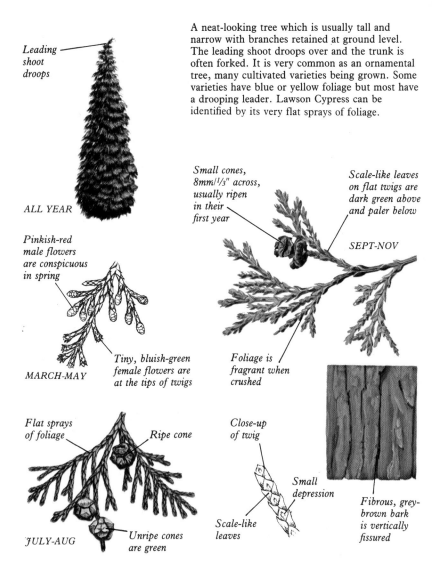

Leading shoot droops

ALL YEAR

A neat-looking tree which is usually tall and narrow with branches retained at ground level. The leading shoot droops over and the trunk is often forked. It is very common as an ornamental tree, many cultivated varieties being grown. Some varieties have blue or yellow foliage but most have a drooping leader. Lawson Cypress can be identified by its very flat sprays of foliage.

Small cones, 8mm/⅓" across, usually ripen in their first year

Scale-like leaves on flat twigs are dark green above and paler below

SEPT-NOV

Pinkish-red male flowers are conspicuous in spring

MARCH-MAY

Tiny, bluish-green female flowers are at the tips of twigs

Foliage is fragrant when crushed

Flat sprays of foliage

Ripe cone

Close-up of twig

Small depression

JULY-AUG

Unripe cones are green

Scale-like leaves

Fibrous, grey-brown bark is vertically fissured

Lawson Cypress

Chamaecyparis lawsoniana 30m/100'
Habitat: Introduced from the western coastal region of the United States of America. Grown here as an ornamental tree or hedge in gardens; rarely in plantations.
Distribution: Common as a tree or hedge throughout the British Isles.
Similar species: Western Red Cedar *Thuja plicata* (p121) has an upright leader.

A neat-looking tree which is narrow and conical when young. Older trees have broad, spreading crowns with a flat top, resembling a true cedar. It has tiny, scale-like leaves but they are not in flat sprays like Lawson Cypress foliage. The cones are larger than those of other cypresses, with distinctive, wrinkled scales. Various cultivated varieties of this tree are grown.

Rounded or flat-topped crown

Tiny, scale-like leaves smell of lemons when crushed

ALL YEAR

Female flowers have curved-back green scales with purple inside

Cones are fairly large, 2.5cm/1" across

Green and yellow male flowers

APRIL-JUNE

Cones take 2 years to ripen

Ripe cone

Scales on cones are wrinkled, with a bump in the centre

Ridged bark is reddish brown on young trees and grey and fluted on older trees

Close-up of twig

Twig is 4-angled, not flat

AUG-SEPT

Monterey Cypress

Cupressus macrocarpa 30m/100'
Habitat: Introduced from Monterey, California. Planted here as an ornamental tree or hedge in parks and gardens. Not grown in forestry plantations.
Distribution: Common in the South and West; rare in highland areas.
Similar species: Italian Cypress *C. sempervirens* has a narrow crown.

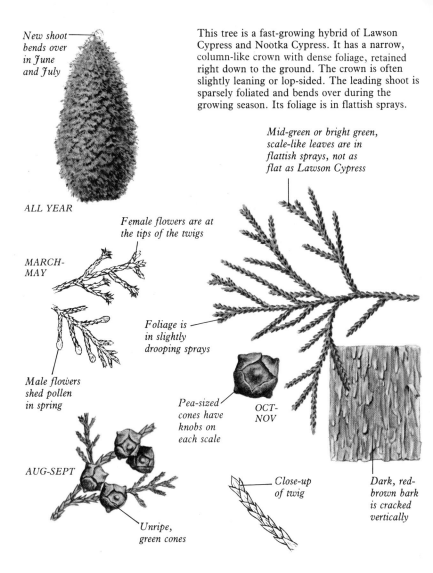

New shoot bends over in June and July

ALL YEAR

This tree is a fast-growing hybrid of Lawson Cypress and Nootka Cypress. It has a narrow, column-like crown with dense foliage, retained right down to the ground. The crown is often slightly leaning or lop-sided. The leading shoot is sparsely foliated and bends over during the growing season. Its foliage is in flattish sprays.

Mid-green or bright green, scale-like leaves are in flattish sprays, not as flat as Lawson Cypress

Female flowers are at the tips of the twigs

MARCH-MAY

Foliage is in slightly drooping sprays

Male flowers shed pollen in spring

Pea-sized cones have knobs on each scale

OCT-NOV

AUG-SEPT

Unripe, green cones

Close-up of twig

Dark, red-brown bark is cracked vertically

Leyland Cypress

Cupressocyparis leylandii   25m/82'
Habitat: Introduced hybrid. Planted here as an ornamental tree or hedge.
Distribution: Common throughout the British Isles, especially as a hedge.
Similar species: Lawson Cypress *Chamaecyparis lawsoniana* (p118) has foliage in very flat planes. Nootka Cypress *C. nootkatensis* has a conical crown.

A narrow tree with a dense, spire-like crown and an erect leading shoot. It is related to the cypresses, not to the true cedars. Old trees have distinctively fluted trunks with soft bark. It can be identified by its wide, flattened, scale-like leaves which have a strong, fruity smell, even before they are crushed.

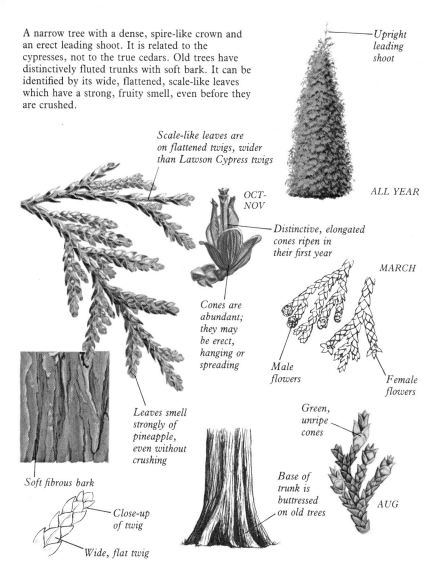

Upright leading shoot

Scale-like leaves are on flattened twigs, wider than Lawson Cypress twigs

OCT-NOV

ALL YEAR

Distinctive, elongated cones ripen in their first year

MARCH

Cones are abundant; they may be erect, hanging or spreading

Male flowers

Female flowers

Leaves smell strongly of pineapple, even without crushing

Green, unripe cones

Base of trunk is buttressed on old trees

AUG

Soft fibrous bark

Close-up of twig

Wide, flat twig

Western Red Cedar

Thuja plicata   35m/115′
Habitat: Introduced from North America. Grown in plantations and in parks.
Distribution: Common as a timber tree in S. and W. England, W. Scotland and in Ireland. Increasingly common everywhere as an ornamental tree or hedge.
Similar species: Lawson Cypress *Chamaecyparis lawsoniana* (p118) has a drooping tip.

Tree form

Bush form

ALL YEAR

This may be a tall, narrow tree, a twisted bush or even a prostrate mat. It has a dense, blue-green crown with upswept branches. It is easy to recognise by its spiky, bluish needles, in groups of three around the twigs. It has very distinctive waxy, berry-like cones which smell of gin.

Needles are scented when crushed

Ripe, berry-like cone

Small, yellow male flowers

Male and female flowers are on separate trees

MARCH-APRIL

Tiny, green female flowers turn blue by late autumn

Green berries ripen through waxy blue to black

SEPT-OCT

Sharply-pointed, bluish-green needles are arranged in whorls of 3

Thin, grey, flaking bark

Berries take 2-3 years to ripen

Common Juniper

Juniperus communis 5m/16'

Habitat: Native. Grows on chalk and limestone in lowland areas and on the acid soils of moors and heaths in upland areas. Not grown as an ornamental tree in gardens.

Distribution: Locally abundant in S. England, N. England, N. Wales, Scotland and in N. and W. Ireland; rarely found elsewhere.

This tree is so distinctive it is virtually impossible to confuse with any other. It is stiff-looking with twisted branches clad in spiky, scale-like leaves. Many old trees are flat-topped with a long, bare trunk. Young trees have branches near the ground. It bears very large cones.

Thick, triangular leaves completely hide the branches

ALL YEAR

Female flowers are usually solitary

JUNE

Male flowers stay on the tree for many months

Large, brown cones grow at the tops of trees; they ripen after 2 years and disintegrate before falling

Overlapping leaves end in a sharp point

ALL YEAR

Smooth, thick, grey bark looks wrinkled

Straight, thick trunk has scars where branches have fallen off

Chile Pine or Monkey-puzzle

Araucaria araucana   25m/82'
Habitat: Introduced from Chile. Grown in parks and gardens as an ornamental tree.
Distribution: Common throughout the whole of the British Isles. Very popular in Victorian times when it was planted in many gardens and in most parks.

An evergreen tree with a dense, broad crown and almost black foliage. It often has a divided trunk. Irish Yew, a variety with upright branches, is very common in churchyards. Yew has very distinctive red, fleshy fruits.

ALL YEAR

Irish Yew has upright branches

Dark green leaves are spirally arranged but appear parted on the twig; they are yellow-green beneath

Male and female flowers are on separate trees
FEB-MARCH

Broad, needle-like leaves

AUG-DEC

Small, yellow male flowers produce clouds of pollen

Unripe berry

Tiny, green female flowers

Foliage of Irish Yew

ALL YEAR

Leaves are in spirals around the twigs, not parted in 2 rows

Fruits are red, fleshy, cup-shaped 'arils'; they enclose a small, olive-green seed

Scaly, red-brown bark peels off in vertical flakes

Yew

Taxus baccata   15m/50'
Habitat: Native. Usually grows wild on chalk and limestone. Planted as an ornamental tree, especially in old churchyards.
Distribution: Native tree is frequent in England, Wales and Ireland, although absent from E. Anglia, Scotland and central Ireland. Commonly planted everywhere.

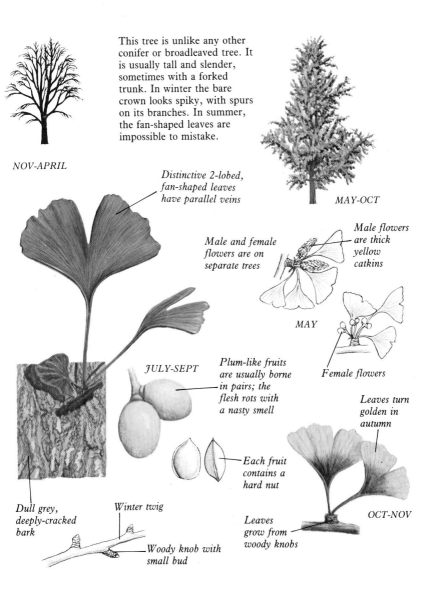

This tree is unlike any other conifer or broadleaved tree. It is usually tall and slender, sometimes with a forked trunk. In winter the bare crown looks spiky, with spurs on its branches. In summer, the fan-shaped leaves are impossible to mistake.

NOV-APRIL

Distinctive 2-lobed, fan-shaped leaves have parallel veins

MAY-OCT

Male flowers are thick yellow catkins

Male and female flowers are on separate trees

MAY

JULY-SEPT

Plum-like fruits are usually borne in pairs; the flesh rots with a nasty smell

Female flowers

Leaves turn golden in autumn

Each fruit contains a hard nut

Dull grey, deeply-cracked bark

Winter twig

Leaves grow from woody knobs

OCT-NOV

Woody knob with small bud

Maidenhair Tree

Ginkgo biloba 25m/82′
Habitat: Introduced from China. Planted here as an ornamental tree in parks and larger gardens. Usually only single trees are planted.
Distribution: Common in S. England; uncommon in N. England, Scotland and Ireland.

Further Reading

Conifers in the British Isles. A.F. Mitchell (Forestry Commission Booklet No.33 H.M.S.O.)

A Field Guide to the Trees of Britain and Northern Europe. A.F. Mitchell (Collins)

Field Recognition of British Elms. J. Jobling and A.F. Mitchell (Forestry Commission Booklet No. 42 H.M.S.O.)

Flora Europaea. T.G. Tutin, H.V. Heywood, N.A. Burges, D.H. Valentine, S.M. Walters, D.A. Webb (Cambridge University Press)

Flora of the British Isles. A.R. Clapham, T.G. Tutin and E.F. Warburg (Cambridge University Press)

International Book of Trees. Hugh Johnson (Mitchell Beazley)

Know Your Broadleaves. H.L. Edlin (Forestry Commission Booklet No. 20 H.M.S.O.)

Know Your Conifers. H.L. Edlin (Forestry Commission Booklet No. 15 H.M.S.O.)

Oxford Book of Trees. B.E. Nicholson and A.R. Clapham (Oxford University Press)

Trees and Bushes of Europe. O. Polunin and B. Everard (Oxford University Press)

Trees and Shrubs Hardy in the British Isles. W.J. Bean (John Murray)

Trees in Britain. R.E. Randall (Jarrold)

Trees in Britain, Europe and North America. Roger Phillips (Pan)

Useful Addresses

Forest and Wildlife Service
22 Upper Merrion Street, Dublin 2, Eire. Write for information on State Forests open to the public in Eire – these include Forest Parks and forests with nature trails and picnic places.

Forest Service
Department of Agriculture, Dundonald House, Belfast BT4 3SB.

Forestry Commission
231 Corstophine Road, Edinburgh EH12 7AT. State forestry authority which manages national forests in Britain. Publishes guides to forest walks, nature trails and recreational facilities on its land. Produces various publications on trees.

Men of the Trees
Crawley Down, Crawley, W. Sussex. Society which aims to promote an interest in and understanding of trees.

Royal Forestry Society of England, Scotland, Wales and Northern Ireland
102 High Street, Tring, Hertfordshire. Promotes education on forestry and good management of forests.

Tree Council
35 Belgrave Square, London SW1X 8QN. Promotes tree planting and cultivation in Britain.

Trees for Ireland
9th Floor, Fitzwilton House, Wilton Place, Dublin 2, Eire.

The Woodland Trust
Ivybridge, Devon PL21 0JQ. A charitable trust which aims to safeguard trees. It plants trees and protects woods, many of which are open to the public.

Index of English Names

Page numbers referring to illustrations appear in **bold type**

Abele **16**
Acacia, False **67**
Alder, Common **24**
  Grey **25**
  Italian 24
Almond **63**
Apple, Common 48, **49**
  Crab **48,** 49
Ash, Common **86**
  Flowering **87**
  Manna 86, **87**
  Mountain **51,** 55
Aspen 17, **18**

Bay, Bull **42**
  Sweet **44,** 64, 65, 85
Beech, Common 26, 29,
  30
  Roble 29
Bean Tree, Indian **90**
Birch, Downy 22, **23**
  Silver **22,** 23
Blackthorn **58,** 62
Box, Balearic 45
  Common **45**
Butternut 21

Catalpa, Western 90
  Yellow 90
Cedar, Atlas **105**
  of Lebanon **104,** 105
  Western Red 118, **121**
Cherry, Bird **59**
  Black 59
  Japanese **66**
  Sargent's 66
  Sour 60, **61**
  Wild **60,** 61
Chestnut, Horse **76**
  Red Horse **77**
  Sweet **31**
Cypress, Italian 119
  Lawson **118,** 120, 121
  Leyland **120**
  Monterey **119**
  Nootka 120
  Swamp **114,** 115

Deodar 105, **106**

Elder **91**
Elm, English **38**
  Smooth-leaved 39, **40**
  Wych **39,** 40

Filbert 28
Fir, Caucasian **97**
  Douglas **98**
  European Silver **94,** 97
  Grand **96,** 97
  Noble **95,** 97
Fontainebleau, Service
  Tree of 53

Guelder Rose 92, **93**
Gum, Blue 84
  Cider **84**

Hawthorn, Common **56,**
  57
  Midland 56, **57**
Hazel **28**
Heaven, Downy Tree of
  71
  Tree of **71**
Hemlock, Eastern 99
  Western **99**
Holly **78**
Honey Locust 67
Hop-hornbeam,
  European **27**
Hornbeam **26,** 27, 29, 30

Indian Bean Tree **90**

Judas Tree **69**
Juniper, Common **122**

Katsura Tree 69

Laburnum, Common **68**
  Scotch 68
  Voss's 68
Larch, European **102,**
  103
  Hybrid 102, 103
  Japanese 102, **103**
Laurel, Bay **44**
  Cherry 44, 64, **65**
  Portugal 44, **64,** 65
Lilac, Common **89**
  Persian 89
Lime, Common **80**
  Large-leaved **82**
  Silver **83**
  Small-leaved **81**
  Weeping Silver 83

Magnolia, Evergreen **42**
Maidenhair Tree **125**
Maple, Downy Japanese
  75
  Field **74**
  Norway **73**
  Smooth Japanese **75**
Monkey-puzzle **123**
Mountain Ash **51,** 55
Mulberry, Black **41**
  White **41**

Oak, Cork 36, **37**
  Durmast **33**
  English **32,** 33
  Holm **36,** 37
  Pedunculate **32**
  Red **35**
  Scarlet 35
  Sessile 32, **33**
  Spanish 37,
  Turkey **34,** 37
  White 33
Olive **88**
Osier, Common **15**
  Purple 15

Peach 63
Pear, Common **50**
Pine, Arolla **112**
  Austrian 107
  Chile **123**
  Corsican **107**
  Lodgepole **110**
  Maritime **109**
  Monterey **111**
  Scots **108**
  Shore **110**
  Swiss Stone **112**
  Weymouth **113**
  White **113**
Plane, American 46
  London **46,** 47, 73
  Oriental 46, **47**
Plum, Cherry 58, 62
  Common 58, **62**
Poplar, Black **19**
  Grey 16, **17,** 18
  Lombardy **19**
  White **16,** 17

Raoul 26, **29,** 30
Rauli 26, **29,** 30
Redwood, Coast **116,** 117

Dawn 114, **115**
  Giant **117**
Rose, Guelder 92, **93**
Rowan **51**

Service Tree 51, **55**
  of Fontainebleau 53
  Wild **54**
Silver Fir, European **94,**
  97
Sloe **58**
Spindle, Broadleaved 79
  Common **79**
Spruce, Norway **100,** 101
  Sitka 100, **101**
Strawberry Tree 44, **85**
Sumac, Staghorn **70**
Sycamore **72,** 74

Tree, Indian Bean **90**
  Judas **69**
  Katsura 69
  Maidenhair **125**
  of Heaven **71**
  Oriental Tulip 43
  Service 51, **55**
  Strawberry 44, **85**
  Tulip **43**
  Varnish 70
  Wayfaring **92,** 93
  Wild Service **54**
Tulip Tree, Common **43**
  Oriental 43

Varnish Tree 70

Walnut, Black **21**
  Common **20**
Wayfaring Tree **92,** 93
Wellingtonia 116, **117**
Whitebeam, Common **52,**
  53
  Swedish 52, **53,** 55
  Wild Service **54**
Willow, Bay **13**
  Crack 10, 11, **12**
  Goat **14**
  Golden Weeping **11**
  Grey **14**
  Pussy **14**
  Weeping **11**
  White **10,** 11, 12

Yew **124**

Index of Scientific Names

Page numbers referring to illustrations appear in **bold type**

Abies alba **94,** 97
  grandis **96,** 97
  nordmanniana **97**
  procera **95,** 97
Acer campestre **74**
  japonicum 75
  palmatum **75**
  platanoides **73**
  pseudoplatanus **72,** 74
Aesculus carnea **77**
  hippocastanum **76**
Ailanthus altissima **71**
  vilmoriniana 71
Alnus cordata 24
  glutinosa **24**
  incana **25**
Araucaria araucana **123**
Arbutus unedo 44, **85**

Betula pendula **22,** 23
  pubescens 22, **23**
Buxus balearica 45
  sempervirens **45**

Carpinus betulus **26,** 27, 29, 30
Castanea sativa **31**
Catalpa bignonioides **90**
  ovata 90
  speciosa 90
Cedrus atlantica **105**
  deodara 105, **106**
  libani **104,** 105
Cercidiphyllum japonicum 69
Cercis siliquastrum **69**
Chamaecyparis lawsoniana **118,** 120, 121
  nootkatensis 120
Corylus avellana **28**
  maxima 28
Crataegus laevigata 56, **57**
  monogyna **56,** 57
Cupressocyparis leylandii **120**
Cupressus macrocarpa **119**
  sempervirens 119

Eucalyptus globulus 84
  gunnii **84**
Euonymus europaeus **79**
  latifolius 79

Fagus sylvatica 26, 29, **30**

Fraxinus excelsior **86**
  ornus 86, **87**

Ginkgo biloba **125**
Gleditsia triacanthos 67

Ilex aquifolium **78**

Juglans cinerea 21
  nigra **21**
  regia **20**
Juniperus communis **122**

Laburnum alpinum 68
  anagyroides **68**
  x watereri 68
Larix decidua **102,** 103
  x eurolepis 102, 103
  kaempferi **103**
Laurus nobilis **44,** 64, 65, 85
Liriodendron chinense 43
  tulipifera **43**

Magnolia grandiflora **42**
Malus domestica 48, **49**
  sylvestris **48,** 49
Metasequoia glyptostroboides 114, **115**
Morus alba **41**
  nigra **41**

Nothofagus obliqua 29
  procera 26, **29,** 30

Olea europaea **88**
Ostrya carpinifolia **27**

Picea abies **100,** 101
  sitchensis 100, **101**
Pinus cembra **112**
  contorta **110**
  nigra subsp. *laricio* **107**
  nigra subsp. *nigra* 107
  pinaster **109**
  radiata **111**
  strobus **113**
  sylvestris **108**
Platanus hybrida **46,** 47, 73
  occidentalis 46
  orientalis 46, **47**
Populus alba **16,** 17
  x canadensis 19

canescens 16, **17,** 18
  nigra **19**
  nigra 'Italica' **19**
  tremula 17, **18**
Prunus avium **60,** 61
  cerasifera 58, 62
  cerasus 60, **61**
  domestica 58, **62**
  dulcis **63**
  laurocerasus 44, 64, **65**
  lusitanica 44, **64,** 65
  padus **59**
  persica 63
  sargentii 66
  serotina 59
  serrulata **66**
  spinosa **58,** 62
Pseudotsuga menziesii **98**
Pyrus communis **50**
  cordata 50

Quercus borealis **35**
  cerris **34,** 37
  coccinea 35
  x hispanica 37
  ilex **36,** 37
  petraea 32, **33**
  pubescens 33
  robur **32,** 33
  rubra **35**
  suber 36, **37**

Rhus typhina **70**
  verniciflua 70
Robinia pseudoacacia **67**

Salix alba **10,** 11, 12
  alba x fragilis 10
  babylonica **11**
  caprea **14**
  x chrysocoma **11**
  cinerea **14**
  fragilis 10, **11,** 12
  pentandra **13**
  purpurea 15
  viminalis **15**
Sambucus nigra **91**
  racemosa 91
Sequoia sempervirens **116,** 117
Sequoiadendron giganteum 116, **117**
Sorbus aria **52,** 53
  aucuparia **51,** 55

domestica 51, **55**
  intermedia 52, **53,** 55
  x latifolia 53
  torminalis 54
Syringa x persica 89
  vulgaris **89**

Taxodium distichum **114,** 115
Taxus baccata **124**
Thuja plicata 118, **121**
Tilia cordata **81**
  petiolaris 83
  platyphyllos **82**
  tomentosa **83**
  x vulgaris **80**
Tsuga canadensis 99
  heterophylla **99**

Ulmus glabra **39,** 40
  minor 39, **40**
  procera **38**

Viburnum lantana **92,** 93
  opulus 92, **93**